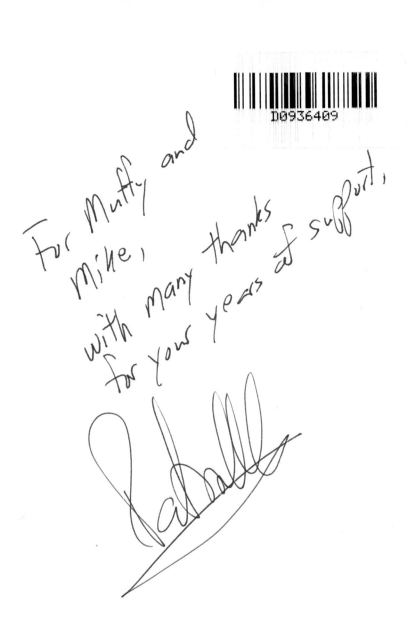

For Muffy and
Mike,
with many thanks
for your years of support,

The Spirit of This Place

THE RICE UNIVERSITY CAMPBELL LECTURES

How Music Illuminates
the Human Spirit

The Spirit of
This Place

Patrick Summers

The University of Chicago Press

Chicago and London

The University of Chicago Press, Chicago 60637
The University of Chicago Press, Ltd., London
© 2018 by The University of Chicago
All rights reserved. No part of this book may be used or reproduced in
any manner whatsoever without written permission, except in the case
of brief quotations in critical articles and reviews. For more information,
contact the University of Chicago Press, 1427 E. 60th St., Chicago, IL
60637.
Published 2018
Printed in the United States of America

27 26 25 24 23 22 21 20 19 18   1 2 3 4 5

ISBN-13: 978-0-226-09510-3 (cloth)
ISBN-13: 978-0-226-09524-0 (e-book)

DOI: https://doi.org/10.7208/chicago/9780226095240.001.0001

Library of Congress Cataloging-in-Publication Data

Names: Summers, Patrick, author.
Title: The spirit of this place : how music illuminates the human spirit /
    Patrick Summers.
Other titles: Rice University Campbell lectures.
Description: Chicago ; London : The University of Chicago Press, 2018. |
    Series: The Rice University Campbell lectures
Identifiers: LCCN 2018021453 | ISBN 9780226095103 (cloth : alk. paper) |
    ISBN 9780226095240 (e-book)
Subjects: LCSH: Spirituality in music. | Music—Moral and ethical as-
    pects. | Music—Religious ethical aspects.
Classification: LCC ML3921.S86 2018 | DDC 781.1—dc23
LC record available at https://lccn.loc.gov/2018021453

♾ This paper meets the requirements of ANSI/NISO Z39.48–1992
(Permanence of Paper).

I dedicate this book to

my dear friend Chris Gwaltney,

a profound spiritual companion

on my journey,

and a helluva lot of fun.

"Oh, come par che all'amoroso foco
l'amenità del loco, la terra e il ciel risponda . . ."
(O, how the beauties of this place, the earth and the sky,
   seem to echo the fire of love!)
—**Lorenzo da Ponte**, from the libretto for Mozart's opera
   The Marriage of Figaro (1785)

What passion cannot Music raise and quell?
When Jubal struck the chorded shell,
His listening brethren stood around.
And, wondering, on their faces fell,
To worship that celestial sound!
Less than a god they thought there could not dwell
Within the hollow of that shell
That spoke so sweetly and so well.
What passion cannot Music raise and quell?
—**John Dryden**, from *A Song for St. Cecilia's Day* (1687)

CONTENTS

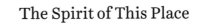
The Spirit of This Place

Music as a Spiritual Force

Spirituality and music are such natural companions that the two words can often, especially for musicians, be interchangeable. Passion for either is infectious. The making of art and the search for life's meaning share common impulses and thus also the same human foibles: both are aspirational; both seek transcendence; both have human practitioners onto whom unrealistic expectations are projected. Both have outlier critics who espouse theories they may not themselves practice. Both provide access to profundity at life's most difficult moments, and both can also lighten us with humor and weightless joy. Both demarcate our days through their association with our most treasured memories.

Music is a spiritual force for one, perhaps too obvious, reason: music is a creation. The few pieces of Western music that are unattributed to a specific author are those that cross cultures, such as the children's taunt "nya-na-na-na-na-nyay!," a little pentatonic musical cell that has existed all over the globe for many centuries, though no one has yet been able to prove precisely why or how. For the rest, the created music, those products of humanities disciplines, a higher human force is at work, the force of creativity and inspiration, and, thankfully, there appears to be no end to it.

We know and study the creators of the great works of Western music. There are endless discussions and disagreements about what any work of art means, but there is no dissent over the claim that Beethoven actually wrote his symphonies or that Mozart penned the operas attributed to him. All of the world's religions revolve, at least on the surface, around the impetus and origin of human consciousness, on why we are here and who created us. There is a humanist tendency to claim that all religions offer basically the same story in different ways, but this is patently untrue, and to suggest so is to insult the memory of the countless millions who have died defending their versions of their faiths, their own preferred origin stories. One chooses to believe one origin story over another, but one doesn't choose to believe that Mahler didn't write his symphonies or Shakespeare didn't write his plays—well, there is continued fringe contention about the latter, but it appears that despite all odds, the Bard did write his own masterpieces. Where belief comes into art is when considering art's meaning: was a higher being responsible for the work of art? Did Bach have to possess a deep religious faith in order to author the deepest works of musical art ever written in the Christian tradition, the *St. Matthew* and *St. John Passions*? Bach, by most accounts, considered himself a craftsman, not the conduit to the divine we now imagine. Yes, he was a Christian, but did his faith write the *Passions*?

Still, all artists know the feeling of handing their work

over to a power greater than themselves. Indeed, that is ultimately what artistry is; it just needn't be handed over to a deity. It just *exists*, separate but inseparable from the person who created it. Verdi's Requiem and Wagner's *Lohengrin* are among the most powerful spiritual experiences in music, but we needn't know anything about either composer's beliefs. What they created exists regardless of what they believe. This is, to me, a powerful spiritual realization, applicable across every sphere of life: we are what we *do*, what we *create*; we are not simply what we *believe* or *say*.

Geist

Music is a *Weltgeist*, and we must be appreciative of the German language's unique gift of compounding words that feel like they belong together: *Welt* and *Geist* mean simply "world spirit," a force of spirituality available to all. *Geist*, often shallowly translated as "ghost," is at the heart of musical humanism. It appears a lot in the culture, as in the term *zeitgeist*, or the spirit of our particular time, or, more paranormally, in *poltergeist*. I prefer to think of music as *Musikgeist*, two words permanently together because they are inseparable. *Geist* has meanings of both mind and spirit and is the thus perfectly suited to describing music and the human spirit. Music is in continual dialogue with us, dispensing its silent and abstract aural wisdom to us; and to lifelong musicians, music always knows more about us than we can ever know about it. There is love of music, a refreshingly common feeling, but there is something rarer, a belief in music as a moral force. Great artists are able to emanate this force, and the emanation should ideally be effortless, though for most it is anything but: in the most extreme personalities, art demands an effort that sometimes ruins lives. If an artist is more at peace with the world, the spiritual force he or she emanates can bring them into closer alignment with nature and themselves, more in love with the wonders of what is around them. When one encounters these artists—and most of them aren't famous because fame isn't what has motivated them—one gravitates to them forever, and they change by perpetuating it spiritual force.

The creation of music is the journey of one soul through itself, and in opera this happens through the musical illumination of a character by a composer. Everything great in opera is, or should be, driven by a composer. Take, for example, just one of the hundreds of arias by George Frideric Handel, "Aure, deh, per pietà," sung by the title character of his opera *Giulio Cesare* (Julius Caesar). The text, by Nicola Haym, is standard eighteenth-century fare, solidly poetic, in simply rhyming couplets and declamatory Italian: "Aure, deh, per pietà / spirate al petto mio, / per dar conforto, o Dio! / al mio dolor" (Ye breezes, in pity / blow upon my breast / to give comfort, O God / to my grief). But Handel turns this text into a Shakespearean-level moment, one of the most profoundly moving of the entire operatic repertoire, at least in the right hands. The idea, once taken as the reason to be a composer in the first place, that a composer actually *crafts* spirituality into a work is now, in our irony-laden world, considered a grandiose idea, though it carries a silent truth within it. We now depend on market forces and algorithms, which are themselves simply our obvious electronic past, to tell us what may fulfill that singular experience we seek in art.

Both the arts and spiritual practices are thought by their

practitioners to have embedded within them a type of truth, a view espoused by the organizations formed to propound them. Both share a tendency to protect their truths, which manifest as "values" in the arts and "beliefs" in spiritual organizations. We are obsessed now with what something is *worth* as opposed to how much it is *valued*, which may well have nothing to do with what it is worth—and this is an important distinction in art. The greatest music, particularly opera, has spiritual force because all art shares a noble goal with spirituality: it gives *voice*. The human singing voice communicates in a mysterious and elemental way. Unadorned and unamplified, singing is simply vibrating air invisibly emanating from within one person and entering another, carrying variously inflected words and ideas with it. We think of great singing as something powerful, strong, and solid, but even without those qualities the human voice is a source of wonder: witness the tenderly moving rendition of the hymn "Blessed Assurance" as sung by Geraldine Page in the film *The Trip to Bountiful*, based on the play by Horton Foote. Page's character, the elderly Carrie Watts, loves hymns and unconsciously hums them. Circumstance has forced her to live in a small Houston apartment with her son and daughter-in-law. The plot of the film involves Watts trying to return to her childhood home—the mythical Bountiful, Texas—and one day she seizes the opportunity to escape. Liberated from the city and once again breathing the country air on her way to her destination, she joyously sings the hymn through the weakness of old age and exhaustion. It is one of the American cinema's most tender and powerful moments.

It is the creative voice of the composer to whom all musicians give their lesser recreative talents. For musicians, the composer is our constitution and scripture, and it is fascinating that in classical music we have parallels to the political originalists and fundamentalists. Just as debates about constitutional documents and religious texts continue to rage — are the exact words of these texts inviolable or are they living and evolving? — some classical musicians view the printed score as sacrosanct and inviolable, while others who see it as merely a rough guide to the content of the music itself, something lying in wait to be unlocked anew with each generation. There can be no full agreement without deep consideration, empathy, generosity, and a collective ability to think broadly and to accept doubt as a human condition. Also, don't expect anyone to get it fully right.

Musicians long for their musical performances to do their speaking for them, thinking, quite rightly, that music is enough. Musicians view the world through the prism of music and an artistic life, or they should, so there is an overwhelming temptation upon receiving any invitation to speak about the boundless complexity of artistic expression, something akin to Shakespeare's description of nature in *Antony and Cleopatra* as an "infinite book of mystery," to try to talk about everything. I'll attempt to avoid that, despite the fact that my creative mind wanders like a puppy — there is just so much! What does music express, and why is expression important? Can an artistic rendering of a feeling ever equal the feeling itself? Or is music so soaked with meaning that it provides a portal to our expressive natures, that which is beyond narrative? Why does music need to express anything? Can't it just be joyous on its own merits? Why do we have to justify arts education by what music can enhance in other disciplines? Isn't it great enough on its own to warrant acquiring knowledge about it? Music's link to nature is easy to see, since so much composed music is a response not simply to the sounds of nature but to the spiritual majesty one can feel in the presence of a mountain, or in hearing morning bird-song in a setting liberated from mechanized sound.

The Rothko Chapel

Visiting the Rothko Chapel near where I live in Houston, Texas, I unexpectedly found myself sitting in its cool, quiet darkness with a girl, perhaps twelve, and her grandparents. In short order, the grandfather said gruffly, "Where are the paintings? Where's the cross? What kind of chapel *is* this?" The attendant and his wife both politely shushed him, but he was still visibly frustrated because the place didn't meet his preconceptions. His granddaughter moved away toward the triptych farthest from the entrance, near where I was, and the light shifted onto the great translucent painting just as she approached it.

She gasped quietly, and I noticed her eyes filling with tears. I silently hoped this family wasn't coping with some tragedy, but the girl's crying seemed more joyous than cathartic. Her grandmother came up behind her and caressed her shoulders. "Well, it must mean something," the elder woman said. The little girl said, unforgettably for me, "It means *everything.*" She got it.

Mark Rothko (1903–1970), who painted the fourteen huge canvases that line the octagonal walls of the chapel, said, "The people who weep before my pictures are having the same religious experience I had when I painted them." They are all dark monochromes that lack a traditional artistic narrative. There is no destination in the chapel but your *self*, and that is simultaneously its gift and challenge—a quality it shares with great music.

The chapel is a liminal and beautiful place, one of my favorite spots in the world and one that I feel lucky to live near. Within its inspirations, over the course of several years, I came to formulate an idea that music is, for many, and certainly for me, a spiritual practice.

But as with our disappointed grandpa, the idea of any art as spirituality would make many immediately think of religious practice, which isn't quite the same thing. For the most gifted people who practice music as well as for those who deeply love it, to even ask the question "Is music a religion?" would be absurd. But if you ask them if it relates to spirituality, almost all, at least in my experience, would say yes, and certainly I would. With this book I hope to illuminate the relationship between art, particularly music, and spirituality.

Music is a spiritual practice for no other reason but that it organizes silence, and it shares many qualities with spiritual practice: for those who love music, it comes with a system of beliefs that they adhere to very strongly and devotedly. It gives meaning to life. It has objects of veneration. It is a cultural system. It has a sacred history. It is social, and its public social conventions differ from its private practice. It inspires solemnity, comedy, gravity, and purpose. Though it involves an absolute science (yes, music is a science), it cannot be understood solely in scientific terms. For it to be practiced at the highest level, knowledge of it must be put aside. Historically it has, like spirituality, been dependent on charismatic practitioners, but its truth doesn't even remotely depend upon charisma.

A moment for what this book is not: it isn't about spiritual or liturgical music. This isn't a book about the history of religious music, nor does it claim expert knowledge of religious practice. Rather, it is a set of abstract ideas, inspired by Rothko's chapel and the diverse reactions to it, about how music illuminates our spirit and how humanity portrays itself most tellingly in its music. Much, but not all, of the music discussed will be operatic because opera is the most complex of the arts, and because opera is narrative drama, with music playing the major role in its ability to bring human beings to spiritual life. Opera is, for its greatest fans, nearly a religion unto itself.

A true musician is not simply someone gifted at making music, but rather someone whose very concept of engaging with the world is sonic. Gustav Mahler, facing Niagara Falls, purportedly said, "At last . . . fortissimo!" This might be viewed as the musical correlation to the young girl in the Rothko Chapel. She just "got it." But no less potent is someone who gets it differently, who musically might be more inclined to agree with the composer Harlan Howard (1927–2002), who wrote country songs such as "The Key's in the Mailbox," "Your Heart Turned Left and I Went Right," and "Pick Me Up on Your Way Down." It was he who defended country music from its detractors by saying, famously, that country music was "three chords and the truth." Even if a composer like Mahler or Wagner is more like two thousand chords and the truth, the spiritual thrill is the same. Musicians love all of it and spend their lives learning about it.

Wondering and Thinking Music

The joyously incongruous and perplexingly inexplicable are regular visitors to daily life in Texas, so they naturally play a role in this book. In 2013, as part of Rice University's Campbell Lectures for the School of Humanities, I delivered a series of lectures on three evenings titled "Thinking Music." This book follows a few of the main themes of those evenings. A lecture, of course, is performance art, so in book form I wanted to isolate what I considered to be its most important ideas, those of arts education and a quick unlocking of music's basic elements—but it was apparent to me during and after the lectures that the main topic was music's spiritual qualities, and that became the focus of this book.

The lectures were designed for that rarity on college campuses now, the humanities student, and thus have a distinctive "first-world" feel. I spoke broadly about culture, as viewed through my own prism, that of a pianist and conductor. The lectures didn't pretend to solve any of the world's problems, nor even the considerable problems microcosmically hidden inside our shrinking art form.

For the purposes of the lectures, I defined the humanities as "created cultural experiences," discussed largely as classical music and opera, but it is my hope that readers of this book can apply the term more broadly. I also define *humanities* in a now-outmoded way: as that which serves to make us more humane, however circuitous our connections to that group of disciplines may be. Caught speeding on the way to a rehearsal one day in Houston, a police officer who looked like Texas's former governor Ann Richards unhurriedly dismounted from her motorcycle, presumably to hand me a speeding ticket. After what seemed like a glacial exchange of both legal and operatic information—for I was late for a rehearsal of a *Don Carlo* production I was conducting—she handed me the ticket and departed. Across it was written, "I like the Giulini recording with Domingo. Have a wonderful performance!" What could more humane than a Verdi-loving Texas motorcycle policewoman with big "hayer" (as they say in these parts) who doesn't give a speeding conductor a ticket?

The thoughts here are, like a creative life lived in real time, full of flashes of information for the purpose of engendering further exploration and thus, by design, are largely incomplete in themselves. My own artistic life is manifested in my work as a conductor of operas and as the artistic director of one of the country's major opera companies, Houston Grand Opera. Perhaps *Wandering Music* would have been a more appropriate title for this introduction, for much of any given day in my vocation assumes completion elsewhere; thoughts will be ignited and people will run with them or not, and the analysis of why certain things work and others do not is one of our constant themes. Conductors, after all, are the only silent participants of a performance; they mutely enable others to make the music while simultaneously making it themselves. Musicians rehearse a hopeful reality, the outcome of which they won't know. Passion is the most ubiquitous emotion in an arts company, and spending it wisely is one of the major challenges of a job like mine, since one of passion's qualities is that it can be blinding. It is a commonly noted paradox that experts are often the very people unable to see what their fields of expertise might be missing.

Privacy

No one could or should tell anyone the spiritual meaning of anything. What is spiritual to you may hardly put a dent in someone else's universe. "The tree which moves some to tears of joy is in the eyes of others only a green thing which stands in the way. . . . As a man is, so he sees" (William Blake, letter to Reverend John Trusler, August 16, 1799). And arts leaders have to acknowledge this while simultaneously recognizing that many people seek the arts for spiritual reasons.

Music is unique among the spiritual disciplines in that it is so abstract. Even some modern painting aspires to narrative; landscapes are still the most depicted visual images. But music of every era is abstract; there is no such thing as "literal" music, despite many attempts to simplify it into a narrow definition.

Why do characters in opera sing? And, further along that idea, what is it about their singing that deepens the emotion?

Words have specificity. We have many dozens of ways to apologize in English, from a simple "I'm sorry" to some utterly abstract connection of a word to an action. But music in opera *is* its spiritual force, the engine of everything about a character and, by mirrored extension, everyone open to experiencing it. Opera is the most powerful of the arts because it is the amalgam of all of the arts; but music is primary among them, and it is music that gives opera its eternal feeling.

Music is a device for unlocking the spirit, as surely as our shins are designed for finding furniture in the dark. We are going to bump into music on nearly any spiritual quest, and even if that isn't the quest we're seeking, music may knock us into it. Music, particularly in opera, often demands that we return to our most childish. We lose imaginativeness and dreamy rigor as we age, sadly. It is the rare adult who maintains a childlike vision of the world and is at the same time able to live within it.

The Touchy Spirit

The idea of the human spirit, for some, naturally conjures spirituality, and in the United States of the twenty-first century, the idea of spirituality often leads directly to that of religious belief. But *spirit* refers to sentience, awareness, access to emotion, and to our unique ability to be conscious of consciousness. It is a human quality of deep importance to the world, and the various semantic permutations of the idea— human nature, culture—can easily erode into simplistic generalizations.

Music is a wholly unique creation of the human spirit. But why is a story told with music often a more meaningful one? How is music able to tell us something words cannot? All musicians know that it does, but how and why does it happen? What is this transcendence?

A work of art need not have spiritual aims or themes to

be received in a spiritual way. This wonderful paradox illustrates the reason for art at all, which is to connect with people wherever they happen to be. My spiritual experience will not be yours or anyone else's. The sharing of passion for one work of art often leads someone to another—and that is the goal of my initiative. It includes a wide range of styles and topics. It embraces works of great religious faith and some that doubt the existence of any creator, for faith without doubt is delusion. It presents works in which composers grapple with the elemental rights of mankind: personal liberty, identity, struggles with the idea of private faith, or the effect of the state on the most vulnerable of society.

Classical music as a cultural force has suffered more change in the last century than other art forms, and each of the myriad complicated reasons could form its own long inquiry and indeed has done so many times. History is always the greatest teacher, whether the subject be spirituality or music, because it does repeat itself: just during the tenure of my own career, roughly the last thirty years, I have seen a lot of change, but what I've seen more regularly is a cycle of such persistent cultural clichés about opera and art in the United States that I'm sure they must afflict all the humanities. Orchestras and opera houses felt beleaguered and hopeless when I entered the industry in the 1980s: traditionalists believed contemporary trends of the era were too populist, while analysts thought the audience was shrinking. Only in retrospect do we view the decade following the American Bicentennial in 1976 as an apogee of both artistic achievement in the United States and of support for and attendance at the arts.

Attendance at classical-music performances in this now golden era was fueled by a preconglomerate recording industry. At the time, record executives were willing to let a commercial blockbuster fund artistically rewarding projects that weren't immediate money spinners but that were important for posterity. No longer: our culture became considerably more oriented toward the immediate bottom line rather than toward posterity. Baby boomers viewed the world in terms of endless possibility because we were raised to do so. But those coming to adulthood in the twenty-first century are so well acquainted with downsizing that they can barely recognize expansiveness. The assumption of cultural growth, the allure of provocation, and the entitlement to happiness were such natural components of American culture that they weren't even named or talked about in my generation until they were endangered.

But what, in spiritual terms, *is* music? The question is rarely pondered even by practicing musicians, perhaps because it is such a subjective, complex, and divisive one. No matter what its content, all art is spiritual to some degree, because the making of art is itself an expression of personal spirituality. But there remains something unique about the nonliteral nature of music and its ability to express spiritual truths, ask spiritual questions, and create cathartic humor or pathos, because the composition of music, while arduous, is a quest for joy and meaning. In this spiritual context I'm focusing on music as it is traditionally defined in the humanities: that which is consciously composed, not simply arranged or copied, and has arisen from the deepest creative impulses of a gifted person, a created experience that heightens and illuminates reality, whether its creator realizes it or not.

What Is Music?

Music as an organized response to nature is as old as other inventions of the human mind and spirit, roughly forty or fifty thousand years according to the current fossil record. We have no idea what music from deep time sounded like, but we have strong evidence that when *Homo sapiens* began to display societal organization, they expressed themselves in various musical ways. The first musical instruments to appear in the fossil record are flutes and drums that were more likely discoveries than creations: wind blowing through hollow, discarded reeds would have logically led to the first flutes, while the plucked tendons of dead turtles made a percussive sound that could be heard for long distances and probably inspired our ancestors' first drums.

The earliest music likely came from the singing voice attempting to be heard over long distances while hunting. Singing and dancing have long been linked, for in primitive human societies nonverbal communication visible and audible from a distance would have been both spiritually expressive and necessary for survival. Many musical forms—galliard, saltarello, minuet, gavotte, pavane, allemande, passepied, gigue, polonaise—are cross-references from the world of dance, and their choreographed steps still dictate their tempos. Today, music is wildly diverse and studded with references from across all cultures and times. There is no single "twenty-first century" music, though there are a huge number of twenty-first century *musics*; our musical languages now are, like the Internet, huge networks of information and influences through which an infinite number of ideas relentlessly pour, a sad amount of it being disposable but the greatest of it being a thrilling fusion of world music.

Music's Basic Elements

Melody is probably the most important element of music for most people. Think of one of your favorite songs and what you most likely recall is its tune. Melodies are formed by creatively organizing individual pitches, or notes. It is pitch, not rhythm, that is the most mathematical of the musical elements. Modern pitch as we know it was quantified and standardized by a mathematician, Pythagoras, but all pitch is a mathematically quantifiable vibration of the air that sympathizes with vibrations in our inner ear. The pitch A, the note oboists play to tune the orchestra before a concert or opera, vibrates at 440 Hertz, meaning that there are 440 cycles per second in the sound wave produced by whatever the source of the sound is—an oboe, a piano, a tuba, or tenor. The sound then travels to you in a longitudinal wave, and you hear it as a pitch. Pythagoras deduced that if the ratio of the sound wave were shortened, the wave would travel faster and create a higher pitch. For example, twice the speed of that oboe-tuning A, 880 Hz, will result in another A an octave higher. Making the wave move proportionately slower, at 220, or 110, and so on, will result in an A at a lower pitch. The human ear is able to discern a range of about eight octaves, up to 3,250 Hz, which is the top A on a standard piano. Producing all of the other notes requires a corresponding set of complex mathematical fractions.

This is rather like diagramming sentences, and, with apologies to linguists, only slightly more interesting. Explaining the mechanics of sound doesn't go very far into actually talking about music, for all of these sounds are organized into an enormous and magical number of musical forms that, like spoken language, speak to us at a more profound level than their origins.

A great melody is a balanced combination of inevitability and surprise, and a superb melody will lead your ear in one direction and then take you into another. Ideas of melody have changed so much over time that older music doesn't always sound melodic to younger ears, no matter how beautiful the textures might be. Certainly, the aversion contemporary audiences feel toward much contemporary music is more specifically an aversion to what they perceive to be nonmelodic. There are, thankfully, countless examples of great melodies, and certain composers were particularly gifted tunesmiths. To discover the qualities of a great melody, one need look no further than the first movement of Franz Schubert's "Unfinished" Symphony, with its gently rolling second theme that so gently dips down, bounces up, and memorably rounds itself out. There are numberless examples of great melodies, particularly by the great melodist composers—Tchaikovsky, Verdi, Dvořák, Schubert, Donizetti, Puccini—or, moving into the twentieth century, Kern, Rodgers, Berlin, Porter, Loesser, and Arlen. Great melodies linger in our memories with ease, but melody is about much more than memorability; it is about an inevitable forward movement.

Melody is perhaps the most philosophically complex and spiritually meaningful element of music, because it evokes the future: it leads and guides. In vocal music it rises and falls according to the dictates of words and ideas. The "purest" music, in nineteenth-century musical philosophy, is melody weighted with its own narrative function, music that doesn't need or want to be attached to words.

Rhythmic notation as we know it was developed in the thirteenth century. Music is obviously temporal; it both organizes time and requires it for communication. A composer generally establishes a pulse to dictate tempo and a meter to organize those pulses, written in various ways at the beginning of a piece of music. Musical sentences of the baroque and early classical eras have an inherent sense of tension and release, of strong and weak beats, that correlates precisely with the rhythmic metrical divisions of poetry and verse.

Musical meter builds long phrases out of shorter and more organized groups, called measures or bars. Music can have two beats to the bar, as in "The Stars and Stripes Forever"; three beats to the bar, as in "Happy Birthday" or the U.S. national anthem; or four beats to the bar, as in a lot of popular songs or carols, such as "O Come, All Ye Faithful." Five beats to the measure is more rare, but the *Mission: Impossible* theme is a famous example. We hear six beats to the bar in the carol "Silent Night," and there are many more complicated meters. Extremely irregular or complicated meters can quickly become very difficult in opera because they can be so difficult to memorize.

The poet Edith Sitwell said, "Rhythm is one of the principal translators between dream and reality." She was talking about poetic rhythm, but it is true for music, too. Good rhythm is vital to any musician, and rhythm takes up a surprising amount of time in preparations for a musical performance, because everyone's inner clock is slightly different. How, for example, does a conductor choose a tempo? This is a complex question in some works, but simple in others. In music from the late eighteenth century onward, composers left very clear tempo markings that they derived from the use of a metronome, and a conductor needs to try to get close to them, if possible, though it is also intermittently fashionable to either ignore the markings or experiment with wildly divergent tempos.

With well-known works like the Beethoven symphonies or Puccini's *La bohème*, for example, or any number of others, conductors over time have tended to either homogenize the tempos, slowing the composers' faster tempos or speeding up the slower ones, or they react against some acclaimed interpretation and try to make them even more of whatever they were supposed to be: even faster or slower than marked. Very few music critics are able to evaluate what they hear based on the score; they tend to evaluate based on their own temporal memory, which may or may not be accurate, as it is for all of us, but their job should be to evaluate as precisely as possible based on a composer's intentions, not their personal preferences.

Harmony is an umbrella term encompassing several other musical elements—tonalities, keys, cadences, modes, polyphony, and modulations—making it the most complicated element of music and the chief area in which tastes have polarized over the centuries between the practitioners and patrons. A melody can be, and usually is, harmonized, though harmony itself is not melodic. Harmony can be very simple or deeply complex, consonant or dissonant, and most often is a combination of all of these; complexity is not the aim, yet great composers can embed incredible complexities and hidden meanings in their harmonic languages.

Most medieval music had a beautifully sparse harmonic language, undecorative and contemplative. Harmony became more regulated in the baroque and classical eras, except that the greatest composers transcended these seeming restrictions with incredible genius. The greatest changes to harmony happened over the latter half of the nineteenth century and stretched into the twentieth.

Another very important aspect of music, nearly a fourth element, is timbre, which is the tonal color of sound. For example, an oboist and a singer can produce the same pitch at the same dynamic, but their timbres differ distinctly. With singers, we will often talk about someone having a "great sound," which usually refers directly to timbre, to the quality of the sound they make. What makes a singer heard in a large theater without amplification is not necessarily the size of the voice, but its natural quality combined with healthy sound production. Timbre gives all musicians a distinctive imprint, a sonic personality, and affects all of the other elements of music. Although a keyboard instrument has a more fixed timbre, it also sounds slightly different depending on who is playing it.

I was made acutely aware of the importance of timbre when I was part of an exchange program to China in the very early days of my career. San Francisco Opera, where I apprenticed as a young pianist and conductor, had an exchange program from the mid-1980s for about a decade, and I went regularly to Shanghai for a wide array of teaching and conducting activities. In 1988 I conducted the first performances of Puccini's *Tosca* produced on the Chinese mainland, in a production variously in Italian and Mandarin, an experience that I treasure and, of course, no matter how many times I conduct *Tosca*, can never duplicate.

On one of my trips to China in those years, I was taken to an elementary-school music class where I was told the children would be singing for me, and they did, with great gusto. First all of them sang together, and then several five-to-seven-year-olds followed individually. I noticed one boy sitting off to the side, not participating, and I asked why. The music teacher, who was very nice and very good, politely told me that the little boy couldn't sing, couldn't even match a pitch, and she didn't want him to embarrass himself in front of a guest. As the class dispersed, the little boy came to my translator and asked if he could try to sing. I said yes, of course, and I played a note on the piano to see if he could match it. The most horrendous percussive sound came out of him, and the teacher tried to shuffle him along. Without thinking about it, instead of striking the piano key I sang to him, and he matched me perfectly, with a lovely juvenile voice. His ear was so sensitive that he was hearing the hammer hitting the string more prominently than he was hearing the pitch it was making. This experience, while ostensibly about timbre, has always stayed with me because it touches on a very important rule for a conductor, or for a leader of any kind: avoid the quick judgment.

The Thin Line

It need hardly be noted that the United States is a religious nation, and although we are far down on the list of countries where residents say religion is important to them (http://www .telegraph.co.uk/news/worldnews/11530382/Mapped-These -are-the-worlds-most-religious-countries.html; also https:// en.wikipedia.org/wiki/Importance_of_religion_by_country), religion plays a larger role in our national politics than these statistics might suggest. Throughout history, human beings have organized themselves into religions with regularity and across every economic and educational background. Despite a majority of people worldwide claiming religious beliefs, only two other regions in the twenty-first century world see a similar prevalence, some may even say imposition, of religion in public life as in the United States: Mesopotamia, the land "between the rivers," now more broadly defined as the Middle East, and maritime Southeastern Asia. This presence of religion in government is part of the national heritage of the United States, but not precisely in the way those on furthest end of the political Right have been trying to impose over the last quarter century, by trying to retroactively impose fundamentalist Christianity onto each of the variously humanist, Christian, Deist, or secular founding fathers.

Though religion is present across all civilizations, only in these three areas does it hold such enormous sway over the governance of nations. In Saudi Arabia, for example, anyone convicted of apostasy is sentenced to death, while this thankfully would be unthinkable under the U.S. Constitution. This is not to say, though, that the United States lacks its moral bafflements: from outside our borders gazing inward, it is difficult to fathom the gun culture of the United States or the type of paranoia that prompts people to create personal arsenals despite an absolutely staggering level of gun violence in our country.

And we somehow manage, despite any moral logic, to justify, for example, the existence of privatized for profit prisons in which prisoners' punishment is bartered by commercial interests, even in states where impartial judges are (another bafflement) elected by popular vote—for how can the law be subject to the vagaries of a vote? According to a Truth-out.org report, "Shocking Facts about America's For-Profit Prison Industry," dated February 6, 2014, this industry, which thrives on the mistreatment of minorities and immigrants, rose by 1,600 percent between 1990 and 2010. We undoubtedly remain a great nation and a desirable place to live, love, and work, but it is also true that many in the United States now recognize a worrisome tendency toward the type of coercion, a demand for precisely shared beliefs, that the Puritans fled in order to come to these shores. It is worth remembering that even the Puritans left because their home country was not puritanical *enough.*

Our discussions of music, which are obviously less importance than those of political realities, are now more often discussions of the lives of a few celebrities: one must admit that this is similar to the discussions among followers of many religious leaders. Religious faith and spirituality are so constantly conflated in the culture now that we've come to take them as interchangeable, yet they are clearly not the same, any more than an arts company is the same as an art, or a map a city.

We are at a time in history in which culture wars continue to escalate, but the term "childish spats" would be more appropriate than "wars," an insult to actual warriors. Our secular democracy, steeped in various Enlightenment-era philosophies and structured on Greco-Roman traditions, is constantly under siege from the noisiest protectors of a few religious traditions across a narrow spectrum of both the Democratic and the Republican party, each claiming "truth," and none, despite wild flights of rhetorical orotundity, behaving in a way that could possibly be thought ethical.

Our spiritual discussions in the United States tend to the juvenile: the policing of the behavior of others, at least until the spotlight gets too close to the one doing the policing, or broad generalizations about the Christian intentions or private beliefs of the authors of the U.S. Constitution. The Internet seems to have given birth to an impressive number of constitutional law scholars in the United States, at least until one breaks what has become the cardinal rule of all online reading: "Do not read the comments section."

Winston Churchill, so often misquoted or misattributed,

did say, "The best argument against democracy is a five-minute conversation with the average voter." This sentiment could be extended into any endeavor, and is certainly true of what can be discerned of spiritual life in the United States by viewing our public discourse about it.

Not Making a Profit

People give money to charity in the United States for only two reasons: to save a life or to change a life. Of course, in recent years an enormous amount of money has been raised and spent on political campaigns, which presumably falls into the "changing life" category; but this is money that could be spent on a great deal else for the public good. But I digress. A great many Americans are suspicious of any art that can't support itself in the free market—why, for example, should a university professor whose specialty is the organ works of Buxtehude be funded by tax dollars, when so few people will benefit from his or her knowledge?

The "market" is endlessly discussed in nonprofit arts companies. Markets of all types quickly become politicized, as they always have. The problem with the "market" in artistic terms is that it can only comment on the past, what did or did not sell within an examined past. It doesn't tell you *why*; it simply answers *what*. Everything in modern life is now commodified; even terrorist groups manage to package themselves for targeted funders. Almost no politician in the United States now will publicly support the arts, for it is considered too politically risky and elitist to do so.

Art isn't inherently aligned with the market, and though artistic works carry moral weight and life-changing moral lessons, their creation and aesthetic impulses follow no inherent moral authority. This may sound like a fantastical or polemical statement, but I truly don't mean it that way: it is simply to say that deeply creative impulses aren't concerned with a moral arbiter like the Qur'an, the Bible, or the Mahabharata. They really do follow their own rules, and this is a hard reality to accept.

Artists aren't funded by the United States government because the government has no need for them, as our governments are now largely built and budgeted for waging war. The pittance which is the National Endowment for the Arts is forever under political attack because it is the easiest way to broadly attack elitism and, by extension, learning itself. Artists are attacked whenever they dare to make political statements, and nonprofit organizations are forever cowering and scouring their activities and communications for terms that might possibly offend someone.

The major threat to art, while always financial, is far and away a cultural and political one. We risk being irrelevant more by not believing in the art itself than by worrying about offense.

There are two opposing views of any work of performance art, and thus any opera: is it set in marble, fixed, and permanent, lying in wait for successive generations to understand it? Or is only viewed differently by increasingly progressive points of view, never fully fixed by the fluid interpretations that change over time? Put any spiritual thought in the place of the art, and you see the immediate correlation: are the great spiritual texts immutable and fixed, or do they change as society progresses?

Arts companies, like other cultural institutions whose products require accomplishment, are now viewed with suspicion by the broader public, seen as places where a chosen few can suture themselves into a privileged evening.

We love to kid ourselves that economic arguments are "true," that because numbers can be quantified and art cannot, that there is more worth in their claim. But created works of art, otherwise known as the humanities, may well be our most precise measure of the past. If one is possible, so is the other.

There is no discernible fairness in the distribution of artistic gifts, and it should be obvious that a marvelous person can be a mediocre artist. The opposite is also true: many people of dubious integrity have been great artists. I use the term *morality* here as synonymous with professional integrity, not in the pious private way the word is often employed.

Unexpected Houston

"I had expected bright colors! So I just looked. O miracle,
peace invaded me. I felt held up, embraced, and free.
Nothing was stopping my gaze. There was a beyond."
—**Dominique de Menil** upon first sight of Mark Rothko's
paintings for the Rothko Chapel, Houston

Houston, Texas, in whose artistic community I work every
day, constantly defies the cultural clichés about it. You won't
read much about Houston in the national newspapers, except
stories about the oil industry and the hundred-year floods
that now seem to happen each year.

By even the most generous standard it cannot be said to
be a beautiful place. Indeed too, much of Houston is a dys-
topian urban horror. The older eastern-seaboard cities of
the United States have a genuine decay brought on by time;
much of Houston's urban landscape is, by contrast, a victim of

either wanton neglect or terrible taste—for instance, the end-less rows of unsightly billboards and telephone poles plunked down in the middle of sidewalks. Cheap buildings that founder in the harsh climate blanket whole neighborhoods, and the income disparity that is the new American reality is vividly on display in southern cities like Houston, as is the painful but inevitable truth that it is the high end of the economic scale that funds the arts for everyone at any other end of the scale. The arts will not be the engine of closing the gap, but it will be the engine of access and the arbiter of the morality of making it all available to as many as seek it.

Too much in Houston, sadly, is poverty, although this city has some of the most ravishing homes in the world housing some of the wealthiest in the country. The bayous that ten-tacle the region—our one citywide shot at beauty—have been largely concreted into submission, removing any sense of their natural flow and inviting a disheartening amount of lit-ter to their shores. On the plus side, Houston is verdant and blanketed with beautiful live oak trees and pine thickets, and the azaleas are wonderful.

Houston became a port city because a group of enterpris-ing businessmen in the early twentieth century decided they were going to make it one, so they dug a sixty-mile shipping channel from the Gulf of Mexico to within sight of down-town, even though the Texas Gulf Coast contained plenty of natural harbors that wouldn't have required such a Pana-manian effort. The channel is one of the wonders of Houston that few Houstonians have ever seen. We have NASA. We have the phenomenal Texas Medical Center—the largest medical complex in the world.

And we have every Houstonian's favorite subject, the weather: "Los Angeles with the climate of Calcutta," as the late Molly Ivins described it. Our winter weather is beautiful, though, and very few people talk about the pristine and temperate days of from October to April, when you can lunch outside and walk or bike everywhere, if you can manage to avoid the armies of leaf blowers, which keep one another occupied by blowing today's leaves back to where they were yesterday.

Colleagues around the world ask me why I choose to live in Houston, and the words always span an octave or two to accentuate the speaker's incredulity. The reason is simple: the people. The human landscape of Houston more than makes up for the lack of mountains and beaches (Galveston is a little over an hour away), and the urban insults are constantly being improved around town: in the past few years the parkways that extend west from downtown have been restored and refreshed and have brought the possibility of urban beauty into the public consciousness, but this too happened because of extraordinary citizens who made it happen, a fact that is also gratefully ubiquitous in Houston's history. Its civic institutions tell the tale: Cullen, Brown, Wortham, Jones, Wyatt, Menil, Law, Beck, Hermann, Williams . . . the names are many but ubiquitous. Houston is about the integrity, generosity, dedication, and love of its people. Those are qualities never to be taken for granted anywhere in the world and they are joyously abundant, surprisingly so for visitors who have already decided what the city might be like before ever seeing it.

We have the beauty of a huge range of arts, and they are vibrant and fascinating in this city built for commerce. Most fascinating perhaps is the aforementioned Rothko Chapel. It is a place of unexpected stillness and reflection amidst the benignly accepted urban chaos, nestled into a quiet neighborhood, housed in an unassuming brick building that you'd easily drive past. The chapel is often a surprise for visitors, as it has none of the traditional trappings of a spiritual space.

It sits, a bit incongruously, in Houston because of a deep-thinking and visionary philanthropist, Dominique de Menil, who instinctively understood that a burgeoning metropolis needed spaces for reflection that were not aligned with any denominational religious tradition. A devout Roman Catholic herself, her artistic tastes and spiritual openness were catholic, with emphasis on the lowercase *c*. Inspired by Yves Congar's lectures on ecumenism that she heard in the cathedral of Montmartre in 1936, she would later recall: "If you want to love and create common bonds you have to understand what makes the other person tick, what his faith is all about. You don't merely respect his religion, but you have a curiosity about it, an awareness" (in Pamela G. Smart, *Sacred Modern/Faith, Activism, and Aesthetics in the Menil Collection* [Austin: University of Texas Press, 2010]). The aesthetic ideal of the city has always been empathy.

The fourteen chapel paintings are enormous, hovering just above the eye line, suspended and aspirational, slightly menacing, somewhat inviting. They have enormous visual energy, yet they invite contemplation. They depict no discernible object or person and are aleatoric, a word born, appropriately enough, in the world of dice and gambling. Until the eye adjusts to the light, they appear monochromatic but aren't. They seem to have no plan, yet they are clearly creations. They can evoke uneasiness and sometimes bring tears from their cathartic beauty. They look utterly different at different times of day. The chapel is completely silent at all times.

I have come to think of the Rothko Chapel, symbolically, as a piece of music, and the perfect symbol of the possibilities of the arts: a secular space in which the self is the only destination. It is fully a creation, a composed and inviting fusion of art and spirituality. It lacks the extroverted spectacular nature of a musical work, but it has a similar, if introverted, aim. I often seek out the silence of the place, and out of that silence often arise musical memories; I'm never sure what to expect. Those associations are what I believe all art to be about, and they go a long way toward explaining to me why music exists, which is that music takes the continuum of complexities of both human life and nature and sings them back to us. Though I always enter the Rothko expecting to hear in my mind's imagination some gentle or contemplative musical memory, often some vast musical gesture appears, like the thrilling hall-shaking *forte* in Aaron Copland's *A Lincoln Portrait* that follows the text "It is the same tyrannical principle," or the great C major sunburst that concludes Rossini's opera *William Tell*, or Siegfried's shattering final moments from Wagner's *Götterdämmerung*. These will mysteriously repeat in my psyche, sometimes for many minutes, until gentler and smaller works take over, phrases of chamber music: the gently rising and falling tune in the first movement of Mendelssohn's Piano Trio no. 1, passed from cello to violin to piano, a melody that never fails to move me, or Lucienne Boyer singing "Parlez moi d'amour," one of the "forever" pieces of music: it seems to have always existed and is indispensable. Over time, the musical forces of my imagination get ever smaller, until I can finally arrive at silence.

And I never fail to remember Dominique de Menil's own sentiments, recorded in *The Rothko Chapel: Writings on Art and the Threshold of the Divine* (Houston, TX: The Chapel, 2010), particularly as I often find myself reflecting both on

arts institutions and the art they are meant to foster and promote, because her thoughts are immediately applicable to our
time and place in the arts in the United States:

> Churches and synagogues are too much like clubs, and as we
> all know clubs are meant to keep people out. Maybe that is
> why so many of the young are staying away. . . . They know
> that we are threatened by economic collapses, police states,
> atomic warfare. . . . The Rothko Chapel could give them hope
> and courage. . . . I see there a series of great encounters which
> would bring together brains and hearts—fresh brains and
> experienced brains, young hearts and hearts enlarged by life.

Practice

No one can make a credible argument that writing or playing music is itself a spiritual practice. It is what artistic expression *shares* with spirituality that makes the relationship between the two a symbiotic one. Religions seek to align themselves with spirituality, but the reverse is not necessarily true: a person seeking spiritual fulfillment needn't find it only in religious practice. Creative artists need not seek spirituality for their practice, but the converse *is* still true.

Only art, or culture, or something "created," rather than "invented," can affectively counter modern cynicism, for since the end of the Cold War, Americans have lacked a faceless enemy on which to project their fears and hatred and have turned instead to an intense, potentially murderous, political opposition. There are those of us who believe, or who believe we know, that art has a major role to play in these divisions.

Music and Spirituality

Does music illuminate something about human spirituality? It feels that it has most often been defined as the other way around—that spirituality is the instigator of music as a human creation.

It feels quite natural to me to turn to music and opera to try to understand something about human spirituality, both within and outside religious practice. A person does not "understand" Wagner, Mozart, or Handel, any more than one "understands" consciousness or spiritual fervor, because artistic works aren't understood, at least in any traditional reading of the word. Even if one understands them as a fine musician might, that doesn't go very far toward grasping their spiritual power. If a work of art is great, then it is lived in and lived through again and again, with generations of engaged sensitivities renewing the work and keeping it alive. Is this not exactly what is done with the vast store of spiritual teachings?

Of all human activities, war has done the most to shape the world. One of the profoundest cultural changes of the last five hundred years, in terms of what it affected and why, caused a great many wars: the Protestant Reformation. We are all free to think anything in the privacy of our own thoughts, but the Reformation thoroughly transformed the public life of the mind in that its changes allowed people to give voice to more ideas without fear of either prosecution or persecution. The truest freedom is that of thought. However, following the Reformation churches became more ideologically pure versions of themselves, and thus less tolerant of humanism. It would gradually return, particularly with the founding of the Jesuit orders in the early sixteenth century.

And then as now, when a group was in need of adherents, they created more icons of their faith (in the arts we call them "stars," but more on that later). More saints created a need for more churches to honor them, and the post-Reformation era was a boom for the building, rebuilding, and enlargement of dazzling sacred spaces across Europe, along with the first large wave of opera houses.

The Counter-Reformation witnessed (but presumably did not cause) the birth of opera and the indeed the need for music as a spiritual force, both within and outside churches. The theatrical focus on the legendary gods of the ancient world placed the truer (at least to the believers) god of the powerful Christian church into sharper relief. The clemency of monarchs was a popular theme, particularly in eras when the monarchs were most corrupt. A few operas, like Monteverdi's *L'incoronazione di Poppea* (*The Coronation of Pop-*

pea), portrayed monarchs as ambitiously corrupt and were considered both scandalous and dangerous public entertainment. As one of the oldest regularly performed operas, *L'incoronazione* now feels, paradoxically, like one of the most modern operas ever written. To twenty-first-century audiences it seems utterly contemporary in tone, for those types of leaders and liars are still very recognizable to us.

Musicians strive to perform beyond notes, to go underneath what can simply be known, all the while recognizing that knowing is never simple. This is the spiritual part of both music and being a musician: the need to go deeper into the art. No artist actually strives for perfection; we just strive to be better.

The Ineffable

There is a perfection of an operatic moment in an opera generally derided now, Gounod's *Faust*, that perfectly illustrates the musical illumination of the spirit within a character. It is not one of the "religious" moments of the work, but rather in its most perfect act and scene, the act 2 Garden Scene, and the moment occurs in a single sentence, a simple four-measure musical phrase: "O silence! O bonheur! Ineffable mystère" (Silence! Joy! Ineffable mystery). The four words are completely standard operatic language for the period, as are the two emphasizing "O"s. Gounod sets the sentence twice, first with a set of ascending major sixths that are answered by a descending version. But it is in the second repetition that the transcendence can come, one of a few in this opera that I believe have kept it in the repertoire and in front of the public since it debuted in 1859. Gounod stretches the word "ineffable" over two measures instead of one, a simple enough musical gesture, one the composer probably didn't think twice about; but in the hands of the right soprano and conductor the effect is magical, the very thing that keeps us coming back to operas again and again. As us usual with opera, the many elements that need to coalesce for this are themselves ineffable: Marguerite's partner in the scene, Faust, must listen to her in the most authentic and simple way possible, without stealing her focus. The lighting must look like the music sounds. There is almost no end to the curious combination of elements that make the scene work for an audience. The scene must illuminate, without anyone being conscious of it, ineffability.

I'm speaking now of a single sentence in a long opera. It is sometimes easier for attentive audiences to grasp these briefer moments in a work, but in the case of some of the most profound spiritual operas or works of classical music, the moments are suspended and heightened. In Verdi's Requiem, Wagner's *Tristan und Isolde* and *Parsifal*, and Britten's *Billy Budd*, the feelings of a transcendent spirituality can extend for hours.

Before there were supertitles, attending an opera meant that many audience members studied libretti before attending, read about the works they would watch and hear, and so were generally more invested in their operatic experience. Have supertitles really revolutionized opera? They have certainly made the work of attending opera an easier experience, and they have unquestionably improved the live experience. But an alternative view is also possible: audiences for all classical music events, including opera, peaked in the late 1980s, just as supertitles were coming into wide use. It could be argued that when the deeper investment of audiences fell away, when they stopped having to do a bit of advance preparation, so did their regular attendance.

As must be obvious, many other factors have also contributed to a smaller audience: the Internet age, which in various ways has made everything available at our fingertips, has lessened our need to attend live performances. But unquestionably, the perfect storm of diminishment of interest has been fueled by the inequity in arts education in the United States.

The Expertrap

I'm a certified expert in one extremely narrow artistic discipline, and only a few hundred people in the world carry a similar expertise, while a few thousand—about 1 percent of the population—have a sustained and active interest in what I know a lot about. My knowledge is thus of little import to the world. Knowledge ultimately teaches you how little you know about anything, and that is the most useful and important thing for anyone to learn, as it gives one an appreciation for expertise in others. We are in a curious netherworld now, in the twenty-first century, in which expertise is derided even as we are ever more in need of it. I am, like any expert, often in conversation with non-experts (that is rather the point of having expertise), and although for the most part these are delightful and passionate conversations, sometimes they are frustrating: non-experts feel expert, and they are bizarrely sure of themselves. I imagine myself on their side, me talking to an expert on something of which I have only a little knowledge, like medicine or sports. Would I argue with such vehemence? Would I insist on the accuracy of my views with the confidence often displayed to me? I don't seek approbation for my expertise, nor do I feel the need to be constantly reminded that I know things. But I feel my knowledge merely creates a hunger for more, so I am always flummoxed when we culturally distrust expertise—when climate science is considered conspiratorial or when people are willing to expose their children to horrendous diseases because they "believe" vaccines are a problem rather than a solution.

Why?

Religious practice seeks to answer the fundamental questions of life. What is existence? What is consciousness, and what does it mean to be conscious of being conscious? Spirituality, in artistic terms, only asks questions; it never answers them. This frustrates the religious, naturally, and has meant that at many times in history artistic expression has been seen not as a mode of spirituality but as its enemy. Asking too many questions is enriching for the human spirit but very hard on religious dogma.

The "spiritual but not religious" movement has a long tradition, and it is a feeling many artists recognize in one another, for we know it when we see it in someone else. This isn't a scientific sampling, but from my experience it feels as though religious faith is generally regarded with suspicion by artists, resulting in questions which are, for artists, completely standard, but which can feel like to the religious like attacks. No doubt the opposite is also true for the religious: some of them probably find artistic expression suspect and feel great wariness when they encounter it. But I've also found that those I consider the finest artists feel that artistic expression is the one safe place for us all to find common ground.

It is not possible to communicate honestly about the spiritual power of music and art without questioning, inquiry, expertise, and openness. Religion should create openness and joy toward the world, yet we see constantly that it doesn't. Yet artists can't claim to have been much better at this, historically: there should be an equal dedication to inclusion and open-mindedness among artists and creative persons, but we also see in them a constant stream of pettiness, territoriality, and rashly formed judgments, the very qualities of which they accuse non-artists. Artists strive for what they don't always achieve, and this is an inherent part of being an artist. Religious practice must be similar: there is an ideal that one doesn't often attain. I can never trust someone who self-proclaims "perfectionism," as there is nothing further from art than striving for perfection. Artists strive only to be *better*, not to be perfect, for it is only the creation that can achieve perfection, not the realization of it. This is, microscopically, my idea of music's spiritual power.

In conversations I have had with people of deep religious faith, there are many parallels and lessons for artists:

1. Don't assume the supremacy of your beliefs.
2. Thoughts aren't facts.
3. No one makes spiritual (or artistic) decisions based on facts; our feelings make our decisions.
4. If your practice, whether spiritual, religious, artistic, or some combination thereof, is not making you more joyful

and open toward the world, you should question why you
are doing it.

5. The only true knowledge is that which leads you to
what you don't yet know. A feeling of knowing all about
something is false.

We are living in a particularly dangerous paradox: more than
half of the citizens of the United States believe that their
religious thoughts are true, that they are actually *factual*.
Others contend that they believe, but that the metaphors of
religious tradition, especially those in the Bible, are not facts
but folklore. There is little common ground between these
two feelings: either the Bible and the Qur'an, or whatever text
embodies one's chosen beliefs, are metaphoric works of philosophy, or they are historical fact; they can't be both.

Enter: arts education.

Our Stuff

One of our most endearingly narcissistic traits is that we believe our era to be one of great change, that everything up to this point in history has led inevitably to the great culmination of, well, us. So it is easy to imagine that every thoughtful person who ever lived has felt that everything current is a decaying version of some better former thing. But it is also true that, culture in the early twenty-first century is changing faster than at any earlier time. We don't even know what our age will be called—perhaps "the age of post-techno-ironic-suspicious cynicism"?

The reflective, creative arts, such as music, writing, and painting, have historically been the quiet refuge of the thoughtful and curious, so we don't yet know what to make of this time of extraordinary technology, particularly that network of networks—the Internet—which is still very new to our world. A youngster born at the outset of the Internet's first broad usage may well still be in college, and few people on the planet ever heard the word *internet* prior to 1992. So the information of our time is unique, and for this reason alone our cultural legacy deserves more of our attention, because it has suddenly become endangered. Culture and art are many things, and they are so broadly defined and often subjective that they can be molded to fit a number of ideologies. One thing is sure, however: culture is never static. Indeed, it eats time with its own relentless accuracy. One of the paradoxes of so much availability of information is that, lacking a basic canon, we often choose less, or even nothing. All of the elements of creation—wonder, awe, dreaming, brilliance, danger—lie within great music. This is spiritual enrichment too wondrous to be lost.

The current unresolved and unresolvable debate in the United States involves religious freedom and the broad inability to see that a separation of church and state protects both equally. A wholesale rewriting of the past should be left solely to creative artists, not to politics or history. But now we see a conflation of art and history, a return to the early days of our republic, when news was chosen or believed, rather than reported and analyzed, and when superstition and myth were prized and rigorous inquiry questioned, instead of the other way around.

What, precisely, does religious freedom mean? Surely true freedom means an ability to choose one's beliefs for oneself. But that's where the new semantic dance begins. One can't choose "the truth," which is naturally what those of the predominant religions claim to hold; but, looking at history combined with human nature, can we ever trust someone who lays claim to the truth? We can respectfully and clearly see a human *need* for truth, but that is surely some distance from claiming to know it. We are in a spiritual crucible now, in which science has answered so many questions and explained so much about *how* things happen, but it can't answer the most important question: *why?* And science, also, has succumbed to human frailty to the extent that it would be nearly impossible to place our spiritual trust in a science that has brought the world a level of unsustainable radiation, which even in accidental overdoses causes only mild outrage. If we won't react to the poisoning of the only place we will ever live, what *will* garner our attention?

At this particular cultural moment, an alarmingly large faction of our fellow citizens want to "take our country back." Indeed, they do—back to 1957–59, the ne plus ultra, in the minds of the most politically conservative among us, of American history. This group feels we are overtaxed, with a top tax rate of 37 percent, although in 1957 the top tax rate was over 90 percent. There is a perception that the majority of people who benefit most from welfare programs are black—a perception that the media constantly supports—while the truth is that most welfare recipients are white. Support for a national social safety net was high from the 1930s through the war years and gained critical mass with the public because of a specific artistic endeavor: the Depression-era photographs of Dorothea Lange, whose gorgeously humanizing photographs of largely white populations in the United States created a sympathetic portrait of our poorest fellow citizens. Lange's poor looked like a downtrodden version of wealthy America, and the images burned their way into mainstream America. Then came the 1950s–'70s, when a permanent imaginary link between African Americans and poverty emerged despite the reality. After the 1960s the vocabulary of racism became significantly more coded and insidious, and we still feel these divisions today. Does art have a role in this?

Our lives either have an aesthetic component or they don't, and it is self-negating to try to create a role for what can't be invented. What will be the future definition of beauty, and how will we provide access to it? I believe that an early relationship with music through arts education is a vital component of a well-rounded individual. I don't naively believe that it is the *only* component, but it has a role as central as mathematics or reading. I believe there must be participatory arts education available to all, not just access to performances on the Internet. Indeed, our digital world, which has made so much available, may well be making us dumber, or at least less curious; we haven't had it long enough to know its long-term benefits or dangers. Orthopedists are already saying they are seeing a change children's posture as a result of their staring down at screens.

In a country that professes to value equality, anyone who bothers to look will see that arts education in the United States is woefully inequitable: wealthy school districts offer a range of arts education across all ages, yet some these districts are only a mile away from a school so poor that it has been forced to choose between a security guard and a nurse. No principal in that position has the freedom to take a stand for the arts. Thoughtful parents are entitled to wonder what will be lost in our country if we lose access to artistic outlets for children in our schools, opportunities for direct learning—painting, playing an instrument, singing, writing stories, dancing. And will we be able to recognize that loss before the adverse effects are upon us? Most Americans no doubt believe that the arts are important, but it is a feeling rarely backed by action. Learning *about* music begins with learning to *make* music. The great flowering of arts education in the 1950s through the early 1980s mirrored the country's postwar prosperity, but the cultural divisions we now feel were growing silently and steadily through that time.

A quarter of a century ago, when Allan Bloom opined in his highly influential book *The Closing of the American Mind* that higher education in the United States had "failed democracy and impoverished the souls of today's students," referencing my own generation, his attack was heard and widely discussed though sadly unheeded, except when it was turned into either a support of one political agenda or an attack on another. I don't know Bloom's politics and don't need to, just as I would far prefer to have no idea about the private religious views of a political candidate. Bloom's points were somewhat hyperbolic in their execution, but his book was full of bull's-eyes. How ironic that a book warning about America's declining ability to think critically has itself been so critically misinterpreted, watered down, and misunderstood. Bloom was instantly branded a culture warrior, with each side seeing in his book the mirror they needed to further polarize themselves. The central point of his book was that the openness espoused by the post-1960s academics led to a "closing," an inability to use the openness of intellectual life to come to conclusions that led to the common good. If everything is relative and all things are equal, where is the need for rigorous intellectual inquiry? Into this breach stepped hitherto relatively dormant political ideologues ready and eager to fill the gap, and they did. But America's cultural fracturing cannot solely be laid at their feet; our current cultural sluggishness is more likely brought on by the new and insidious technologies that surround us.

The Internet age, and particularly that of the smartphone, is slowly killing long-form works of art in ways we have yet to fully analyze and recognize, and many believe the realization will come too late. We communicate more often within the newly acquired vocabulary of social media than by the older forms of conversation and artistic communication, which feel foreign in the 2010s. Rather than creating devices to enhance our thinking, we are beginning to alter the way we think to more closely mimic *them*. The language of the Internet— "connection," "availability," "wired," "downloading"—has become our new lexicon of communication, another industrial revolution. We assume connection because we can now be virtually present in more than one place, but of course, this splitting is creating a lack of *actual* presence, a lack of availability—the opposite of what we intend. Our attention spans have shrunk, not because of the ubiquity of information, but because of the tyrannical devices to which we are connected. Our smart phones do not require a critical eye from us, and we needn't be mindful when we engage with them. A few scientists and psychologists have claimed that the digital world is simply evolving along with our brains to a twenty-first-century level, but artists take a different view: the digitized life is alienating us from our selves, distancing us from the very art that was created out of our depths to mirror and guide us.

As the world has gotten more crowded, it has become more important to me to regularly seek out liminal spaces, those few spots in the world that seem to possess a spiritual dimension. In the United States we are in one sense more connected than ever, have more access to more information than in any previous time, yet many of us are experiencing great spiritual unease. Because there is so much to choose from, do we choose less? Musicians self-reflect all the time, because mastery of music requires one to spend a huge amount of time with one's own limitations. Music is one of the self-teaching arts and can't be mastered any other way, yet it needs no mastery to be enjoyed.

Iniquities of Inequity

The spiritual implications are strangely clear: we need to exercise some control over the media's domination of our minds, or at least we need some instruction on how best to use it to our intellectual advantage. Can one defend a position that music is even part of an answer to the problems facing us in the twenty-first century? The world is complex, and there is no single key to managing modern life. But I do believe that a basic knowledge of great music has a role to play in our spiritual lives.

A lot of knowledge about a subject can, if one isn't careful, take away a lot of joy in whatever drew one to it in the first place. This is true of more than just music or art, of course; it is also true of spirituality. Opera, as an art, is a complete absurdity at any practical level, and the deeper one goes into the extravagant expense of even the smallest-scale projects, the easier it becomes to just give up. Knowledge about anything gives us a wider view, and it is incumbent on artists to use that wider view empathically, to view and share the deepest aspects of our art, to always ensure that we are accessible to all, that every student of every class and race and economic condition has the chance to learn about art and all it can teach us. Arts education isn't remotely equitable in the United States; generations have chipped away at its importance. Yet the arts are the essence of freedom, so if access to art isn't equitable, we are falling far short of our potential as a culture.

Inequality is a reality, a result of either our past inaction or unfortunate but deliberately made decisions. Inequity, though, is more serious, because it implies intent, a sense of moral superiority on the part of the privileged. Talent is unequally distributed, of course, but we must ensure equity: that access to the development of whatever level of talent an individual possesses is available to all. Spiritually, do we provide equitable access to the full range of human spiritual practices, so that people experience true freedom, the freedom of choice? Obviously not: the overwhelming reason people choose one spiritual or religious practice over another is geographical, not philosophical. We fight inequality, but that is only the surface. Inequity is the presence of unfair advantage and an absence of opportunity, and our constant vigilance against both is needed going forward.

Inequalities may always exist, but if the culture itself doesn't see it as inequity, then the problems will persist. It is impossible to have true freedom without equitable access. How does this relate to spirituality? If access to spirituality is similarly inequitable, or if spirituality is solely relegated to religious institutions, with no competing ideas or few available secular ideas, what does this say about freedom?

Maintaining some control over technology is as much

about preserving personal identity as it is about preserving culture. Concerns about technology are nothing new, of course, but the need for space apart from technology, for reflection and simply some breathing room, is ever more vital as we move further from a cultural canon and from knowledge that is not available at the press of a button, but which one acquires through reading, lectures, and, most profoundly, conversation. I deal with this nearly every hour of my day as an artistic leader, so constantly that I feel the same must be true for leaders in any field: how do we share the passions of our lives by using dispassionate technology? Technology has enabled a spiritual disconnection from culture, and this has created a vast amount of hidden anxiety across a huge spectrum of our lives.

Dead White Guys

The classical canon has traditionally been, like so much else, celebrity driven; however, the greatest celebrities of classical music share a unique characteristic significantly different from those who are prominent in other art forms. They are all dead: Monteverdi, Bach, Handel, Gluck, Haydn, Mozart, Beethoven, Donizetti, Liszt, Bellini, Verdi, Wagner, Mahler, Berlioz, Tchaikovsky, Puccini, Rachmaninoff, and too few others. Furthermore, they are all creators. In all other cultural fields of the twenty-first century, celebrities have largely been performers, re-creators rather than creators.

Nationalism has played a huge role in the promulgation of classical music. Music by composers from the traditional Old World nations—Germany, Hungary, Austria, France, Italy, and Russia—makes up the basic canon of classical music. The English-speaking nations—the United Kingdom, Canada, Australia, and the United States—have historically been defined as having musical traditions that copied those of the Old World. Most other countries, speaking broadly, have generally been consumers of classical music rather than creators.

And this nationalism persists in the idea that someone from a particular country has a special affinity for his or her native music. This does little more than contribute to the idea that there are important and unimportant musical destinations, a clear message that art is for the privileged, a place to which one must travel instead of having it be an integral part of our lives, wherever we may be. The global village that is so obvious in every sphere of today's culture is almost nowhere to be found in classical music. Artists long to believe that music is the international language, but our musical nationalism defies this. If art is for all, as we claim to believe, then what is considered great in Salzburg will be considered so in a small town in Wyoming.

Righting the Unwritable

Rigorous reviews of the performing arts, those that ignite dialogue among patrons and from which artists can learn something, are sad rarities now, with so many newspapers downsizing and reprioritizing and opinion and criticism being so conflated, as though they were the same and equal practice. Newspapers are more apt to cover the antics of celebrities than the art itself, and this is likely a permanent condition. The most common "reviews" artists receive are ones they never see, for they are done by fellow artists privately reporting back to their institutions, though some appear in various anonymous forms such as blogs. Obviously, no credence can be given to an anonymous opinion, but standard-free blogging is the wave of the immediate future, even if blogs have served few of the higher purposes of criticism, the primary of which is to foster dialogue. Bloggers largely attract those already in agreement with their premises and preconceptions.

If I could offer advice to young artists on the subject of being criticized, it would be this: your detractors will not be swayed by good reviews, nor will the affection of your admirers be altered in the slightest by a poor notice. And if you are in any type of leadership position, don't imagine you can be an effective leader without offending someone; it is the nature of leadership that you will have to make decisions that won't and can't please everyone.

Spiritual dialogue, too, can so easily be stripped down into talk about a particular belief or tenet of a faith, simplified and generalized down to the sharing of a simple list of what one believes rather than as a paradigm for how to live. Such dialogues can leave anyone outside their faith wondering about the purpose of belief at all: if it does not make one more compassionate and loving toward the world, more joyous, what good is it? If spiritual life is simply about spending time with others who believe precisely as you, about ticking off a set of behavioral boxes, or if your practice is simply about the policing of the behavior of others, doesn't that greatly diminish the spiritual depth of life? In spiritual terms, the Internet makes it possible to never have one's views challenged, to rarely have to embrace doubt. Does this not weaken beliefs? Why are there now over thirty thousand different denominations of Christianity, a third of which have arisen in the past twenty years, the years of the Internet? And the number is undoubtedly far greater, as many churches in the United States refuse to be regarded as denominations at all, declaring themselves uniquely the "true" church. Are the theological delineations so great and the differences so vast as to require so many different interpretations? Sources vary widely on the precise number, and this is obviously a subject too vast for this book of this size—and furthermore, one that places me in danger of creeping away from my topic—but the situation is so eerily similar to that of arts groups in this second decade of the twenty-first century that we would be delusional not to make a connection. In fact, it is illuminating to sometimes exchange the words "religion" and "art"—or "religion" and "music"—for that can clarify the way we sometimes rearrange our prejudices and fool ourselves into thinking we are thinking.

Music is always greater than any words about it can be, but great musical descriptions bring spirituality to mind in that they traffic in poetic or metaphysical themes, stating truths without interpreting them, taking delight in the very existence of a thing. Take, for example, Theodor Adorno's description of the finale of a Mozart piano concerto. Even if one does not know the work being described, one can practically hear it from Adorno's words; if one does know it, he so effortlessly and joyously describes it that it makes you want to pull the score off the shelf and play it:

> That closing section in the finale of Mozart's A major Piano
> Concerto [K. 488]: a mechanically varied accompaniment
> figure between tonic and dominant over a pedal-point, with
> a melody which really only advances like the ticking of the
> second hand and then, without changing direction, suddenly
> breaks up into the most minute motifs; that conclusion whose
> dense texture brings the whole development and dynamism
> of the rest of the movement to an end, as if the framework
> wished to take prisoner the time that had flowed freely
> earlier on. What a close resemblance to the clock which the
> seventeenth-century philosophers imagined to be the nature
> of the universe. This was the clock which a Divine Mechanic
> had originally set in motion and then left to its own devices,
> trusting in the efficiency of the mechanism. It is a magic

mechanism. While controlling time itself, by incarcerating it, it displays the time to an unknown observer outside. Inside, everything remains the same. The world is the dream of its sleeping Maker. But when the clock of Mozart's closing section, the coda, starts up for the third time, it is as if the Maker had suddenly remembered His half-forgotten work, as if He had intervened and broken the spell. Time takes control of the clock and, reconciled, plays its epilogue to itself before falling silent. (*Quasi una Fantasia: Essays on Modern Music*, trans. Rodney Livingstone, 1992)

This is a beautiful and loving description of music in a style that would likely be now considered orotund. But it leaves us curious to experience the music. It is analytical and precise. It brings a spiritual dimension to a work that has no spiritual intent, at least that we know of. It is, like Mozart's concerto, utterly devoid of irony or cynicism, and Adorno gives himself over to the feelings of the work. Why is this so rare now?

The Journey

It is the creation of music, not just its reproduction, that is the journey of one soul through itself. In this time in which irony is so prevalent and cynicism so celebrated, grand thoughts and symphonic ideas are defined as grandiose. We now depend on market forces to tell us what may affect us, what may fulfill that singular experience we seek.

And, alarmingly, social media, so new in our culture, teaches us to react quickly and without reflection. In 2014 National Public Radio broadcast an April Fools' Day piece entitled "Why Doesn't America Read Anymore?" The content of the story explained that the headline was an experiment, the whole thing a joke, and asked the reader not to comment. Sure enough, though, thousands' of comments ensued, pronouncing at varying levels their indignation at the headline's supposition without reading the content. We see this played out every day: social media turns what we should want to be a face into a mask.

Technology has now supposedly made possible a secure wall against stress, a way to make life simpler, but it isn't real. The stresses of life can't be faced by a device; they have to be faced by a fully engaged spiritual human being. Technology hasn't relieved the stresses of our lives; it has greatly multiplied them: As I'm sure many others have experienced, I've sat through entire plays, films, concerts, and meals in the presence of people whose attention never left their phones. Attending a memorable performance of *Parsifal* at the Royal Opera House, Covent Garden, a woman in front of me texted throughout the entire performance. Ushers tried to stop her. She refused. Her fellow patrons tried to admonish her. She refused. Everyone finally gave up and put what attention we could back to Wagner.

Technology has given rise to a virulent type of individualism insidious enough that it does not yet have a name—narcissism doesn't cover it, but it is related—in which the digital world effectively disguises itself as inclusive in the world it enables us to share, but we are making fewer choices than before because of the availability of so much information. Digital opinion, "the comments section," has given us the illusion that all opinions should be accorded equal weight, which in any cultural pursuit simply isn't true. But digital thoughts allow for little to no confrontation with opposition and present a longer-term danger to the world, because thoughts *feel* like facts.

Are there solutions to the cultural dangers of this digitized world? There are many, and although they are unproven and unscientific, artists will swear by them because we experience them every moment we spend practicing our craft.

Music, not as spiritual practice but as a spiritual force, can most fully pierce the shield that protects the self. Surveying the depth and diversity of artistic creations in the world, it is difficult to escape the feeling that music is the deepest of man's cultural pursuits. Arts education at the primary-school level is key.

The World of the Imagination

"I believe in intuitions and inspirations. . . . I am enough
of an artist to draw freely upon my imagination.
Imagination is more important than knowledge.
Knowledge is limited. Imagination encircles the world."
—**Albert Einstein**, interview with George Sylvester
Viereck, *Saturday Evening Post*, October 26, 1929

Reading the United States Constitution, particularly the Bill
of Rights, solely from an artist's point of view, one is initially
struck by the overwhelming beauty of the language. Then the
most important elements emerge: the centrality of the individual, though never at the expense of the many, and the
preservation of the liberty of thoughts and ideas. This is particularly important when we reflect on what a full artistic education is capable of achieving as an integral part of a well-
rounded curriculum. Musicians know, because they practice

it every day, that while they are utterly dependent on the collaboration of others to practice their craft, they must also have full command of their own talents and skills in order to be a member—a "citizen"—of an ensemble. The moment this basic participatory trust is breached, all manner of irritating problems ensue, performance is poorer, and the art itself is degraded in the eyes of both those who practice it and those who experience it. Several key issues regarding the presence of a deity in public life stem from recent history, from the 1950s, as a response to Communism. "In God We Trust" was added to U.S. paper currency only in 1957, ninety-six years after the United States first began printing paper money. The Pledge of Allegiance, written in 1892, did not include the text "under God"; that was added only in 1954, sixty-two years later. And the motto of the United States, "E Pluribus Unum" (Out of Many, One), was adopted by an act of Congress in 1782; only in 1956, 174 years later, was "In God We Trust" added to the Great Seal.

It is important for cultural discussions now, when Americans are more likely to align themselves with like-minded groups that rarely challenge them, to note that the centrality of the individual as a national philosophy was an essential characteristic of being American throughout the early years of our republic, enshrined with poetic beauty by Emerson, Thoreau, Whitman, and many others. The sociologist and civil rights activist W. E. B. Du Bois lived a particularly eventful and inspiring ninety-five years: he was born just after the Civil War, in 1868, and lived through both calamitous world wars of the twentieth century and into the dawn of the civil rights movement, dying in Africa in 1963. There surely has never been a more passionate or erudite advocate for educational equality. Throughout his life, Du Bois was, sadly, fighting for equal rights between the races, and although we may hope that the darkest part of this history is behind us, it is worth remembering his struggle as we see the new and insidious racism of the twenty-first century—insidious because the digitalization of opinion has allowed it not to have a face.

Reading Du Bois's beautiful 1903 book *The Souls of Black Folk* from the vantage point of more than a century later, in an America Du Bois could never have imagined, how can we not think of the current state of arts education? We can now look through his statement, beyond his unique prism of race, and still see huge inequities:

> I sit with Shakespeare and he winces not. Across the color line I move arm in arm with Balzac and Dumas, where smiling men and welcoming women glide in gilded halls. From out of the caves of evening that swing between the strong-limbed earth and the tracery of stars, I summon Aristotle and Aurelius and what soul I will, and they come all graciously with no scorn nor condescension. So, wed with Truth, I dwell above the veil. Is this the life you grudge us, O knightly America? Is this the life you long to change into the dull red hideousness of Georgia? Are you so afraid lest peering from this high Pisgah, between Philistine and Amalekite, we sight the Promised Land?

Beyond the obvious realization of how far our beautiful language has drifted from its possibilities, we have the profound spiritual beauty of his sentiments: that knowledge is the only true freedom, and its value lies in simply possessing it. My deep concerns about the loss, or at least dilution, of arts education ultimately have less to do with music or art than the full life of the mind and the extraordinary combination of unrealized possibilities to which we have become inured. We sit in our noisy world and watch inequities float by like balloons, but with the assurance that leaf blowers will blow them away to someplace where we won't have to see them.

Is One Person's Noise Worth More than Another's Silence?

I wonder if we realize just how much extraneous noise most of us are regularly exposed to, and just how harmful it is to our psyches?

I have extreme noise sensitivity, enough to probably be a syndrome of some description. Because I make my living with my ears, it is hardly surprising that I experience some sensitivity, but what I physically feel when faced with unnecessary noise goes beyond, I think, the normal paradigm. Intentionally noisy restaurants, those designed for maximum "buzz" with additional loud music added to the mix, are physical torment for me: I become nauseated and unable to enjoy anything about the experience, unable to eat, unable to converse with friends. Construction noise, even blocks away, triggers in me a huge spike in anxiety for reasons I can't quite fathom. Construction is inevitable in any urban environment, and the logical part of my mind knows that; but the terror I feel when approaching a construction site is irrational. It is all about the noise.

Leaf blowers send me into spasms of horror, and I have to get away from the sound as soon as possible. When they begin in my neighborhood, I jump in the car and get as far from them as I can. I know every brand of ear plug available on the market. I marvel at people who can go about their daily lives amidst the constant din.

Leaf blowers are easy to identify as noise pollution, since the unfortunate people who have to work with them every day often have to wear industrial-strength ear protection to guard their own ears. Would that those of us nearby had the same opportunity! But what of the other noise nuisances to which many of us are regularly subjected? Cellular phones have erased any sense of sonic distance from strangers, so we all now have to cope with hearing the private conversations of others in inappropriate places. Conducting Mozart's *Così fan tutte* at the Metropolitan Opera in the early 2000s, just at the outset of the widespread use of cell phones, a patron right behind me got a phone call during the performance *and took it*. As it happens, the man must have been a veterinarian, because everyone around him, including me and most of the Met Orchestra, were subjected to a conversation about a dog's kidney operation. This went on for many minutes, with seemingly no one thinking it the slightest bit unusual.

The breaking of the sonic barrier has extended beyond phone calls, however, in that the decibel level of many conversations now, especially among the young, has increased beyond comfort. Countless times I have gone to a coffee shop or bar just to read a book, only to have the experienced scuppered by some screaming quartet of youngsters. No one expects large cities or large gatherings to be silent, but what is new is the level of inappropriate noise; the idea that some conversations are to be private, and that when you are in a public space your voice can be regulated to a quieter volume, seems to be permanently lost.

Why, for example, do airlines choose to make such noisy choices? Flying is already an assault on most of the senses, but we additionally have to endure utterly deafening flight announcements that send many of us covering our ears because they are many decibels over what is necessary. Then the inflight snacks arrive, and instead of something silent or easy to open, the food arrives in loudly crinkling packages that aren't only noisy to open, but whose noise multiplies as patrons eat, and multiplied again by the hundreds of passengers. There is a quieter and more elegant way to achieve snack time on a plane, but the noisier option is taken, presumably because it saves money.

Not even driving in a closed car can ensure silence. Drivers will play music at a volume dozens of dozens of decibels higher than what is safe for both their driving and their auditory health. Why do people think it is suitable to subject everyone around them to thumping "boots and cats and boots and cats and boots and cats" beat-box noise against our will? We've grown so immune to noise pollution that police often don't even bother to take calls for violations of the laws against it, simply because such violations are so prevalent now, the laws so laxly enforced, that they wouldn't know where to start.

I prize silence. And silence is expensive, when by rights it should be noise that is expensive, not silence. I hope that exposure to and knowledge of great music will make us all treasure the sounds we seek, and will help solve the growing problem of endless noise, which takes such a high psychic toll on all of us.

The Biz

As I have already mentioned, the music industry itself is quite
a different animal from the art form, no matter how deeply
all artists want them to align. The price of immersion in any
industry is exposure to its basest elements, and the tiny world
of classical music is not immune to it. In fact, it is probably
more susceptible to bad behavior because of the relatively re-
mote possibility of making a lifetime career in it.

It is lazy to opine that we are simply in a cultural decline
and that culture has always waxed and waned, a truism that is
of little consolation when you have only one life to live, as far
as we know. We must be able to view our artistic selves as mirrors of the culture at large, and to examine them with honesty,
in much the same way that we owe it to our country to be patri-
otic. The two worlds parallel nicely for our purposes: shallowness and empty platitudes make me equally uncomfortable,
whether they are about patriotism or art. I believe in a deep

love of one's country, a full and respectful type of love, but also a fully adult love that recognizes faults, discusses them, and tries to have a transforming effect on them. So much patriotism in the United States now, like many defenses of the arts, feels infantile and shallow, idealistic and overprotective, unable to see beyond a particular yoke, and disproportionately indignant at anything less than total admiration. We forever seek out as adults that which comforted us as children, and there is little in life of more value than authentic knowledge and authentic idealism, the real stuff of dreams.

The most profound connection to music is only to be found in the making of it. The next best is to be in the same room with those making it, with no encumbrances or enhancements. A distant third connection is listening to music on a device. We must convert a larger portion of our arts institutions to the goal of education, not to protect the futures of our organizations, but because of our civic duty to share what our arts can offer to modern life. We cannot expect that any future government is going to do it.

The Russian painter Wassily Kandinsky, in his essay "On the Spiritual in Art," was most eloquent on music's spiritual qualities:

> Music is the most instructive art. With some exceptions and
> deviations, music is an art which never uses its media to make
> a deceptive reproduction of natural phenomena. On the con-
> trary, music always uses its own media to express the artist's
> emotional life and, out of these media, creates an original
> life of musical tones. The artist who sees no point even in
> depicting nature artistically and, as a creator, seeks to effuse
> his inner world into the outer envies music—the most non-
> material of all the arts—in its facility to attain this aim.

The idea of the human spirit, for some, conjures solely religious belief. But *spirit* is actually a reference to sentience, to awareness, to the accessibility of emotion and intellect, and to our unique human ability to be conscious of consciousness. It is unlikely that our cherished canine and feline friends spend much time pondering how they arrived at their existence.

In 2014 an Associated Press poll found that more than 40 percent of Americans are "not confident in the theory of evolution," and nearly as many doubted the planet was billions of years old. That we can't yet know whether its age is 4.6 or 4.8 billion years should not lead us to assume we know nothing. Discussions of the spirit and faith are often similarly reduced to greeting-card platitudes, lacking depth and inquiry, and can diminish a part of our lives that wants and needs expansion. Our natural world, reflected in our art, is wondrous and dazzling and also too complicated to know fully, yet national dialogue about our own natures is absent, and our commitment to educative tools that enable the search of that knowledge founders when it is reduced to a simplistic belief in one paradigm over another.

Empathetic thought and action are becoming more and more rare; indeed, actions no longer appear to be the focus of American religious practice. Rather than providing a guide to living, religion in America seems obsessed with the sharing of specifically articulated beliefs. Music does not assume simplicity, and neither is it bettered by complexity, so art's role in all of this is to recognize that facts and statistics, important as they may be to science, have little effect on how people make decisions in their lives. It is a great paradox that we can scientifically prove that facts don't matter and emotions do, yet that fact would also be refuted by those who question science! Art and spirituality share a deeply important characteristic: their ultimate purpose is to entice the individual to self-reflection. Yet this, too, is at odds with the more common feeling of the twenty-first century, in which we tend to rely less on our own reflections and more upon our identification with groups—political bodies, congregations, or groups of like-minded souls in which our views will likely be unchallenged—to form our opinions. This is a curious condition in a democracy such as the United States, founded as it is upon the central importance of the individual. The theatrical analogy may be useful here, again, for theater involves a group of people who must work together to achieve a common goal, a performance, though there are undoubtedly thousands of disparate opinions about how to get there and why. If a basic arts education can instill even a portion of this idea, and we know it can, can we really afford to be without it?

We know music to be a wholly unique creation of the human spirit. But why is this so? Perhaps music makes nothing happen besides itself, as the most curmudgeonly claim; but because everything and its opposite are always simultaneously true, music could just as easily be proof of some greater human dimension, a spiritual force that is beyond our ability to understand, but which the wonder and mystery of music allows us to touch for brief moments. Music as an art, whatever the genre, is a spiritual unlocking.

A work of art need not have spiritual aims or themes to be received in a spiritual way. This wonderful paradox illustrates the reason for art at all, which is to connect with people wherever they happen to be on their spiritual journey. My spiritual experience will not be yours or anyone else's. Passion for one work of art often leads us to another, and often our astonishment, or bafflement, about what someone has chosen or written, is the very thing that leads us to it, or gets us near it through something else.

Why is a story told with music often so much more meaningful? Why do characters in opera sing, and why is it so moving when they do? Music, as a purely metaphorical language,
can't depict literal images except in the most banal ways.
Words have a specificity that music does not. We have dozens of ways to apologize in English, from a simple "I'm sorry"
to some utterly abstract connection of a word to an action.
However, music has an emotion power that words lack. It can
take the idea of an apology and transform it into a spiritual
breathlessness it could never achieve with words alone. Think
of Count Almaviva's apology to the Countess in the final moments of Mozart's *The Marriage of Figaro*: there can be few
moments of contrition, either in art or life, so beautiful, so
real, so touching.

Aren't all cultural pursuits spiritual to a degree? They are,
but there are works of art, particularly in larger forms, that
beg us to examine ourselves more fully, that invite spiritual
quests, or that symbolize them more completely than others.
A great deal of time in the cultural arts today is spent in ana-
lyzing the reasons young people no longer seem interested in
larger works and in reworking our activities to fit the shrinking attention spans of millennials, as though nothing can be
gained from the past so that the world needs to adapt to their
needs and ways of learning. But what about the spiritual loss
of arts education and of the introspection it invites? There
are long-form works that have a depth and greatness that
simply can't be learned in a superficial way, and they invite a
much closer look at the world.

I have a deep feeling that Bach's *St. Matthew Passion* is
the greatest single work of musical art. This is an admittedly
subjective feeling, one I have examined throughout my life,
and through this work (although not exclusively) I have examined my own spiritual priorities and beliefs. I do not fol-

low the precise faith that is the subject matter of the *Passion* itself. Indeed, I have struggled for many years to transcend the feelings engendered by the religious teachings from my youth that did not eventually align with my adult spiritual beliefs, a common and healthy feature of adult life. Yet my feelings about Bach's creation have only intensified through my life, something I relay solely as a shared thought that might instruct rather than as some unsought confession. Are my feelings the result of a deeper spiritual sensitivity on my part, or a deepening ability to recognize artistic greatness based on my experiences in an artistic life? The distinction is important, for it is likely one or the other and not both; but it is also appropriate and desirable for me to identify, privately, the source of my feelings. The *St. Matthew Passion* is great solely because its own creator, Bach, reacted with empathy and artistic truth to a text. He crafted it out of his imagination, a miraculous thing. Whether the performance we experience is good or bad or mixed, the creation is there. The *St. Matthew Passion* was the culmination of a tradition of musicalizing the final days and hours of Jesus Christ. In the earliest known versions, a celebrant chanted the story. Later, other characters were added, as Gregorian chant gave way to polyphony and an expanding vocabulary of dramatic musical devices to tell the familiar tale.

The *Passion* was composed for a single programmatic purpose, for a single Good Friday service in Leipzig. He wasn't writing "for the ages," just for a single day, April 11, 1727, in the life of the Thomaskirche in Leipzig. Many believe Martin Luther's 1519 treatise on the Crucifixion gave Bach the creative impetus for this *Passion*, and many have felt the need to align Bach's personal beliefs with his artistic achievement in this greatest of Western musical works. But, ultimately, is it necessary for us to know anything about Bach's own beliefs to be moved by the *Passion*? No.

Nature has no beliefs, only knowledge, and thus no need of us. If humankind were to mysteriously disappear today, the world we inhabit wouldn't notice. It would simply, and quickly, restore itself to a natural balance that we have briefly interrupted. The majority of people believe we were invented or designed by a higher power, but as we exist amidst a natural world that follows its own physical laws and forces, with no regard for any other laws, does it not seem possible that we invented and designed God? This doesn't, for me, diminish the greatness of the concept of God.

For the entire known history of humanity, nature has been more eloquently honored in art than in our physical stewardship of it. Nature has the last word on everything, and in this, too, we emulate it with both the high arts and with our spiritual traditions: we assume that if we mirror nature's assertions of "truth," we will somehow be taking a stand that will make a difference in the world, as though we are somehow able to fully understand nature's laws, which we currently don't and never fully can. Those artists who have made a permanent mark on the world are those who went uncompromisingly into the world and made their statements, against all odds and logic. In our media-soaked world, it is assumed that artists who achieve fame have achieved success, as though notoriety and accomplishment were interchangeable, rather like our conflation of democracy with capitalism. There is no telling any of them apart anymore, because the decline of the arts in the public conversation, in the very imagination of the world, has meant that nuance is a major casualty. *This isn't, naturally, the only reason.* It is of grave concern to artists that fame and accomplishment are so often confused, because that lack of discernment, which is a nuisance in art, is a precipitant danger to public life: when political candidates can be elected simply because they can devise more memorable phrases than their opponents, that is an extreme danger to the world. And when spiritual leaders can remove personal responsibility from spiritual traditions and focus on the behavior of others, the potential comfort and catharsis of those traditions is similarly eroded.

There is so much we can never understand, and that feeling is bound to expand in the coming years as more and more information becomes available on our devices. But the creations in which we engage in real time and which emerge out of silence are the only ones capable of reaching further into us. No matter how much simplification we try to impose, the world around us is immensely complex and interconnected. Representations of nature, of emotion, of all of the strange experiences of history have been the great unique testaments of our existence that we leave behind. Music is the art best able to invite us not just to know it, but to feel it. This is a precious thing, to be treasured, and we must not let it slip away.

Indefinable Malaise

In these early years of the twenty-first century, a general worldwide pall has descended on classical music, particularly opera. Many in our new era view the performing arts as the holdover of a ruling elite, implying that the art is either meaningless or that its artifice is an inherent fraud in a world in need of deeper solutions to the plethora of problems it faces. Confronted by worldwide water shortages, grave health concerns, global climate change, and the now constant threat of terrorism, who can possibly defend the "felt" experience? Threats to arts institutions are everywhere. If the dangers were solely financial, they would be easier to identify and cope with, but the more challenging aspect is cultural: the arts play a significant role in freedom of thought, and simply because the role can't be quantified in numbers is no reason not to protect it; indeed, is the very reason *to* protect it.

Baby boomers, those of my generation, were raised in a

time of cultural expansion and fully expected this seemingly limitless burgeoning to continue. We now recognize this as a feeling unique to our generation; the current generation leaving college does not feel it, and that realization has unquestionably hit the parents with whom many of them are still living. Is it for this reason that we now seem to prefer comforting cultural reassurance over challenging curiosity? Or that we are more apt to identify with groups that reinforce our prevailing views rather than challenge them? Or that, despite living in an era in profound need of expertise on all technological and creative levels, we as a nation have dangerously politicized knowledge itself?

There is a prevailing view today that classical music must change or die, that all of the paradigms that have been accepted as true should be thrown out; but this view entails many assumptions, the greatest of which is that our institutions are the same as our art. My friends who are spiritual leaders, of diverse traditions, report similar trends. There is now such a widespread distrust of institutions and of expertise that people feel willing to throw it all out in order to give preference to a void.

In the professional arts world, in ballet, opera, and symphonic, visual, and theatrical companies, there are endless discussions about how we should transmit our art form, how "live" it needs to be, how large the permanent forces should be to deliver quality performances, how much moral responsibility a company has to keep the largest numbers of artists employed versus cutting jobs to free up funds in order to reach more people, how to respond to cultural trends, and, inevitably, how much artists should be paid. The prevailing discussions are always inevitably financial, as that is where nearly all discourse begins and ends now. But the larger questions, the ones that must be recognized, tackled, and faced down, are not fiscal; they are philosophic, artistic, and, I believe, spiritual. These questions are best answered privately, but the profession and the times expect public declarations. There are such deep truths embedded within the classical art form that artists feel they must be transferable to every sphere of life, cultural or otherwise. The Internet, however, has brought us a world in which everything is assumed to be public, even though there remain many moral and ethical questions that can only be cherished in private—because the glance upon them changes them negatively, like chemicals that change their properties when they are observed.

For many—including, surprisingly, many practicing artists—a successful arts institution is one that most cunningly maintains the status quo; others believe that institutions should be maintained only to the extent that they stretch the boundaries of the form. Arts leaders are both the custodians of an art and the visionaries of its future, and although those two roles don't always sit politely together, achieving a balance of them becomes the job, which is itself a balance of artistic and fiscal concerns. What if, as many now think, the regular work of large arts companies is simply a backdrop against which the uncompromising work of others can be viewed in relief? Must it all be set afire, Wagner-like, in order to maintain the warmth for just a little longer?

Arts boards quite rightly seek sustainability models and strategic plans, yet these corporate models don't meld easily with what art continually tells us it needs: expansion, energy, freedom, innovation, and risk. Listening to the voices of art may seem a fool's errand in light of the issues facing the world now, for what can music credibly say to a terrorist? But it is also true that the world is made more pliable and creative only by the solutions and innovations created in its art.

The current cultural shift away from the classical arts in

the United States is seismic indeed, and it can't be accurately measured in ticket sales. There is a feeling of inhibition and caution in arts institutions in the United States now, particularly in the larger ones, albeit with a huge sense of gratitude to those generous few individuals who keep them running, but also with an accompanying awareness of the differences in economic class between the funders and the consumers. Musicians continually seek their fair share of the scarce resources and, in the case of an opera house, inevitably view the spending of those funds on scenery or costumes as a misplaced repurposing of limited assets. Competing ideologies constantly collide in arts companies, for they are microcosms of the larger world in which they function. Just as we see in political ideologies, operatic artists can easily splinter into various factions:

Opera singers believe that productions should focus solely on them and on the relationships among the characters. They are not wrong.

Stage directors think that opera productions should provoke, innovate, step outside of tradition and expectation. They are not wrong.

Conductors believe that theatrical conservatism preserves the fidelity of the composer's creation. They are not wrong.

Smaller arts groups feel the larger organizations crowd them out of the competition for precious arts dollars. They are not wrong.

A museum curator wants to gather the best of the world's holdings into a single show attractive enough to draw a crowd, while a museum director wants to strengthen his or her own museum's holdings. Both impulses require huge resources. Neither is wrong.

Directors of ballet companies want audiences for their

evenings of mixed repertoire, cognizant that their repertoire of popular story ballets is frustratingly small: *The Nutcracker*, *Cinderella*, *Romeo and Juliet*, *Swan Lake*.

Theater companies now have to hone their missions down to minutiae in order to carve out their piece of the pie. The broad-repertoire theater companies—those that balance classic plays with new works, comedies with tragedies, the provocative with the comforting, musicals with plays—are dwindling and splintering into smaller divisions.

And the list goes on. The dearth of repertoire to which the public will respond is a persistent and worrisome problem that is rarely spoken of. Here again, we encounter an element that changes if it is observed too closely. I believe that what is true in opera is true in other art forms, and is thus true across a range of cultural pursuits, including spirituality: the world is turning away from "repertoire" as a concept, away from a canon, and toward a fused idea of art, a new *Gesamtkunstwerk* that is decidedly different from the artworks of the past, in which the traditional repertoire will undoubtedly play a role, albeit a changed one.

Spiritual practices differ from spiritual organizations in precisely the same way arts organizations are variously aligned with the arts they are meant to promote. The goal is for the art and the institution to be tantamount to the same thing, just as churches always believe themselves to be inseparable from their beliefs. But institutions tend to be less disturbed by history's larger forces than by a simple inability to find agreement within. Look at the vast numbers of denominations within particular religious traditions, often separated by impossibly minute differences of their basic beliefs. The very existence of denominations implies an agreement about the collectively worshipped deity, yet there is not even agreement about *this*: the sheer numbers of "gods" identified in our traditions, with each denomination believing it to be "true," defies even the shallowest logic. But this, too, is where invented culture and spiritual practices align: facts, as defined by those who don't share a certain belief, are of no importance whatsoever to either, because it isn't the factual that is being sought in them. We all feel the fallibility of human institutions played out in our daily lives: in the arts we simply have ego and/or insecurity filling in for the deities (to the man with the hammer, everything looks like a nail). Temperance is mistaken for weakness, and intolerance is mislabeled as decisiveness. There are surely endless lessons in these sad alignments, for arts companies, too, have splintered into ever finer niches, often solely because of the personalities involved.

Composers craft spirituality through large-scale musical architecture, through the calculated and inspired integrations of music's qualities: rhythm, harmony, melody, and timbre. The greatest musical works have a feeling of inevitability from start to finish, of musical material that grows from small musical cells into a logical conclusion. Britten's *Billy Budd*, for example, has an overwhelming sense of arrival and ethical summation in its final moments, but only because Britten sculpted this, perhaps unconsciously, into the larger harmonic design of his opera. Audiences are most likely unaware of these associations, but they sense the completion and tautness of a work if they are open to long-form storytelling.

The Grand One

Music is the primary defining element of opera because of its
ability to illuminate all of the arts' profusion of complemen-
tary elements. This is a potentially profound spiritual lesson:
our twenty-first-century world unendingly focuses on the narrow and the literal, and to deeply examine such an abstract art
as music within a context of more literal elements—words,
drama, design, and so on—will hopefully bring us closer to
some conclusions about the role of music in our lives. Opera
is many things, but at the spiritual level it remains what it has
always been: a telescopic enlargement of human emotions
that allows us to see under their surfaces. Opera is spiritually
attractive precisely because elements of it are so purposefully
unreal. Seeking verisimilitude in an art form in which people
communicate through singing is to seek the literal in what is
metaphorical and imaginative (though many try!).

The purposeful separation of spirituality from religious

practice in art is motivated by one of the sadder realities of twenty-first-century life: the natural world as reflected in our art is wondrous and dazzling, but it is also too complicated to know fully. Yet there is no national dialogue about our own natures, and our commitment to educational tools that would help us to learn about them is grounded in infantilism, reduced to a simplistic belief in one paradigm over another. Art's role in all of this is to recognize that facts and statistics, important as they may be to science, have little effect on how people make decisions in their lives.

Quote

Music, like spirituality, is deeper than any discussion about it could ever be. Unique among the fine arts, music is mysterious and unquantifiable, beautiful and unsettling, yet is based on completely quantifiable mathematical principles. Music's abstract qualities are thought to be universal, but mathematical principles are more completely so: they hold true in every culture, at every altitude and weather condition, and in every political climate. This is not true of all of music's subtleties, at least in practice. Mathematics and music share the beauty of a majestic inner logic that contributes to, but doesn't define, the outward wonder they evoke. As with mathematics, knowledge of music creates more of itself and can lead to that vital and much more important destination beyond knowledge: to the imagination.

Music is notoriously uncooperative to write about. Words do well in elucidating the science of music but not so well in clarifying music's art, what it means, what it is for, why certain pieces of music are better than others. Our egalitarian culture, which assumes that either anything famous is great, or that everyone's opinion, informed or not, is equally worthwhile, is also at odds with discussions of art.

Our tiny classical profession is often charged with elitism, and often we deserve the indictment: a quick glance at cynical, gossipy classical music blogs, or the country club atmosphere of some performing arts organizations (even some that claim inclusiveness and diversity), or the lifeless writing of most of the few music critics who are left, can leave artists feeling that there is a distance, a chasm even, between the ennobling art we love and the ignoble and/or aphoristic way we so often communicate about it.

Does spirituality bring happiness? It is often thought to, but the evidence for this belief is spotty. Music is thought to bring or at least enable happiness, but this idea is belied by the lives of many musicians who find a great disconnect between behavior and aspiration. In the arts of the 2010s there is a culturally unmoored feeling that rather than being poised for artistic expansion, we are in danger of losing some deeply important human expression. This manifests in endless discussions about our institutions, as though they were themselves the arts practiced within them.

The Artist Apollo and Company

Perhaps theory is compelling because there is such fascination with those who transcend it. Theory is thought to be a
dry pursuit, but the spiritual elevation inherent in the study
of theory needn't and shouldn't be. Each of us has our own list
of transcendent creators with whom we particularly connect
and creations we would take to a desert island. Shakespeare,
Handel, and Mozart would easily top my list, along with Bach,
Cézanne, Emily Kngwarreye, Yourcenar, Emerson, Hesse,
Verdi, T. S. Eliot, Britten, Sondheim, and Tennessee Williams. They form the basis of my personal canon, and there is
no question that I view the world through a prism created in
part by each of them. It is through them that I have been led
to a huge array of other artistic ideas, and it is through them
that my own creative awareness, my spirituality, has unfolded
to me like a labyrinth: I entered in and moved through it, with

new challenges and inspirations being constantly presented. Passion for one artist led to dozens of others. Over time, some fell away, while others would come and go. My thoughts were more temperate and considered, and I became aware that although my thoughts felt true, felt like facts, they weren't. They were simply mine. Could this be true of all art, and is it thus true of spirituality, I wondered?

In art, for every truth there is an opposite truth, like the four quadrants of a Chartres labyrinth. Surely, then, one must reason, this is true for everything: that everything and its opposite must be equally true. In opera, one composer is particularly associated with that idea—the most controversial and compelling figure not simply in music, but in recent Western art, Richard Wagner.

Why is this? Every possible artistic ideology can be projected onto Wagner and find support, which is why he seems to be the perfect metaphor for the twenty-first century. This extraordinarily expansive artist, about whom more has been written than any other, was a gigantic professional contradiction: a "pure" artist with abhorrent personal views, an ennobling creator who in his ignoble personal life rarely rose above the behavior of a spoiled juvenile, a composer of rare gifts who considered himself a poet. The nineteenth-century philosopher Friedrich Nietzsche worked very hard to quantify and explain the artistic mind and the forms of creation, and he is credited in modern philosophy for outlining, in his *The Birth of Tragedy from the Spirit of Music* (1872), the dueling artistic concepts of Apollo and Dionysus. Although Nietzsche was hardly the first to identify the concept of dichotomy, his ideas have had enormous influence over creative thought ever since. One of Nietzsche's chief struggles was his inability to explain or describe Wagner. Wagner did not fit the paradigm of Apollonian and Dionysian art; he sat thoroughly outside of it, as he does still.

Performing musicians, the vast majority of whom are re-creators, are generally Dionysian, a reference to the Greek god of wine, and thus of intoxication and pleasure, while creators—composers, writers, and painters—are largely Apollonian, an allusion to the god music, who is associated with balance and order. Apollo demands distance and freedom from observation; he is independent. Dionysus thrives on close proximity and loves being observed. True creators, Apollos, are rare: they often feel either like a conduit of some greater vision, sometimes even surprised at what they create; or, conversely, they will feel thoroughly like craftsmen, detached from their creations, observing them with a separate self. The Dionysian, however, feels unified with the self, is capable of deep joy and melancholy, and is comforted by being a part of a larger unity; he feels the effects of the Apollo's creation. The Apollonian will be more solitary and reflective, pragmatic. Apollo will build walls to protect against nature; Dionysus will enjoy the chaos of the storm.

Wagner, paradoxically, would probably have disapproved of the cult of personality that has surrounded the performance of his works, because he viewed them as transformative experiences that aimed to alter the world's view of itself by returning to our epic storytelling roots. Wagner thought man to be immortal, with our nearest earthly glimpse of redemption to be found in a woman's love. In an 1864 article, "On State and Religion," he wrote: "To the religious eye the truth grows plain that there must be another world than this, because the indistinguishable bent to happiness cannot be stilled with this world, and hence requires another world for its redemption."

Wagner's operas musicalize several important philosophies and spiritual traditions; his final work, *Parsifal*, combines Buddhist with ancient Christian elements. Wagner was steeped in German and Nordic epic literature, in which, as a young man, he found his boundless passion. He spent the remainder of his life realizing those early visions, often at tremendous cost to anyone in his path. His theatrical ideal was the ancient Greek dramatist Aeschylus, whose own works were presented in the context of a religious festival, a format Wagner emulated and created in a theater of his own design. This theater, Bayreuth, which he built in the south German state of Bavaria, is still devoted to playing Wagner's works exclusively. Any discussion of Western musical harmony uses as its nodal point the second measure of his opera *Tristan und Isolde*, in which a single chord unmoored traditional harmonic rules. Musicians and critics powerfully project a great deal onto it, with many blaming Wagner for stretching the boundaries of music so far in his compositions that he left little room for innovation to follow.

But the opening of *Tristan*, to Wagner, was simply an expression of a larger idea, a distant spiritual awakening into which we emerge. To him it had none of the overwrought tensions of its later associations, over which he obviously had no control. He wrote, in a letter to Mathilde Wesendonck, that the famous prelude to the opera represented to him simply the Buddhist ideal of the beginning of the world. The harmony was only a means to an end, not a thing in itself, and that is the first and most important spiritual lesson that music teaches: each of its elements is a spiritual metaphor.

The Gravity of the Decline of Arts Education

The decline and loss of arts education in primary and second-ary schools should be of grave concern to everyone, yet it often is sidelined by seemingly more pressing matters. It would be comforting to call it a "contentious" issue, for the situation would not be nearly so dire if there were any contention about it. Instead, we have silence. No matter that the issue is of high import for the nation, and not just for artists: in no other sphere of education is economic inequity more apparent than in the arts. We live in a time of great educational uncertainty, brought about by the political divisiveness that pervades every attempt at civic progress. How can I defend the teaching of the arts at a time when the United States ranks twelfth in world literacy among the Western nations, twenty-fifth in math, twentieth in science, and perhaps most shockingly, fifty-first in life expectancy at birth—and this from a nation that verbally rededicates itself to upholding high educational standards every election cycle? (My source for the rankings is Pearson Education, © 2000–13, at www.infoplease.com. The life expectancy ranking came from the website of the United States Central Intelligence Agency's *World Fact Book, 2013.*)

We have few facts to prove that arts education is vital to a democracy, yet qualities vital to society are uniquely taught by a basic knowledge of music, particularly singing, literature, poetry, dance, and visual expression. These are all arts whose truths lie within their practice, and their inherent storytelling qualities are as important for children as subjects more recently deemed to be, ironically, "common core."

Any artist is, sometimes to a fault, familiar with that quality most essential to critical thinking—doubt. Editing or molding reality to fit into comfortable existing ideas won't work for artists, who by the nature of their practice must constantly adjust their personal realities based on what their artistic disciplines are telling them. With rare exception, musicians make music with others, which necessitates empathic communication and an openness to having one's assumptions challenged. A great musician is prepared and confident, to be sure, but a musician who has no doubts about his or her own prowess or ideas cannot be a great musician. We cannot prove that a group of schoolchildren who learn to play instruments, sing, write stories, and paint will improve society, but any thinking person can imagine that those pursuits can help our young people become vital players in the immensely complex world in which we now find ourselves. The future is going to depend more and more on creative solutions, and therefore on minds trained in that creativity.

The most vital elements of American greatness have historically been our educational system and our diversity, yet at the time of this writing we appear to be witnessing a wholesale dismantling of American education. Ethnic diversity has been the common denominator of all great historical cultural flowerings. Vienna, London, Paris, New York—each slowly took on layers of complexity because of their wildly diverse populations. Music is an artistic manifestation of human diversity, because it comes from the world's cultures and their influences on each other, and because it is practiced so widely. But without arts education at the primary-school level, equitably distributed across all economic and social groups, we are unlikely to experience a cultural renaissance.

If this feels like a grandiose claim to lay at the feet of arts education, consider what is required to learn the basics of music, to name just one artistic discipline, when it is combined with participation in a disciplined ensemble:

1. The initial work of learning about music isn't about dogma or testing; it's about creativity and challenging one's assumptions. One can learn the basics of music with a team, yet unlike the "testing is everything" zeitgeist of modern education, the competition is only with oneself.

2. In art as in an authentic life, there are no shortcuts. Mastery of an art takes practice, a valuable lesson for children to take into adulthood. Despite the constant rhetorical flourishes from both political sides every election cycle, we are seeing fewer and fewer students reach adulthood with the creative training that the new occupational sectors will demand. We are in a technological time requiring great expertise all around, yet we have allowed a distrust of expertise and practice to overtake our country's greatest asset: our tradition of secular public education. If we lose this, or if it deteriorates further, it threatens our freedoms more

than any of the distractions that are now so prevalent. Athletic education is also important—nothing is more vital than good health, and participating in team sports also teaches many important creative tools—but only a limited number of students can participate, and the competition, even at very young ages, can isolate and demotivate. The arts aspire to be more democratic and inclusive, and they teach private responsibility and discipline; a large ensemble needs the energy of everyone's expertise.

3. Passion is one of the hallmarks of childhood, but the adult sharing of passion is an acquired skill. Teaching children to hold onto their juvenile passions—not just their interests but their passions—teaching them to choose ways to think, is a pathway to adult happiness. Passion is an awareness of the beauty and power around us, and learning what has meaning and what doesn't can be taught through a broad arts-based education.

4. Music has options. The language of music is not absolute. It teaches creativity and critical thinking because any musical phrase can credibly be played countless numbers of ways. Great music has an inherent truth, but the truth is inside, not on the surface. Learning this is at the heart of adult success.

The Elusive Art

> "The orchestral conductor should.... possess ... almost
> indefinable gifts, without which an invisible link cannot
> establish itself between him and those he directs."
> —Hector Berlioz, "The Orchestral Conductor" (1855), in
> *A Treatise on Modern Instrumentation and Orchestration*

Several prominent conductors in history have laid down guidelines for themselves and others of their profession, many of which are currently ignored because they fight so strenuously with the *Geist* of our moment. Richard Strauss was an acerbic and rather revolutionary young man, a hothead who, like every composer of his generation, emulated Wagner. He was a superb conductor, as can be easily seen on video, though he was clearly the antithesis of the modern "performing" conductor: there is footage of him conducting his own "Presentation of the Rose" sequence from his opera *Der Rosenkava-*

lier, one of the most aurally ravishing moments in Western music, and a passage that generally sends conductors into paroxysms of heaven-gazing emotion, yet its composer conducts the sequence with a dispassion unthinkable today. If we didn't know that this is the man who wrote the opera, much of the opinion machine of today would pronounce him lacking in commitment and far too detached from the performance. It is worth noting, though, that there is no doubt in this passage about any of the information a conductor exists to convey: when, where, and how. There is no personal imposition of his personality in his conducting, even for music he created. He is following his own first dictum of conducting: "Bear in mind that you are not making music for your own pleasure, but for the pleasure of your audience."

Some of Strauss's rules are pithy in-jokes for musicians, such as never looking at brass instruments lest they play too loudly—though Strauss was largely right on this point, and many of my colleagues break this rule every day. The most interesting rule he sets down involves two specific operas of his, and it deserves a little unpacking. He instructs conductors to conduct *Salome* and *Elektra* as if they had been written by Mendelssohn, "like Elfin music," referring, of course, to Mendelssohn's famous incidental music for Shakespeare's *A Midsummer Night's Dream*. What is the meaning of this curious statement, and what does it mean for a conductor? A particularly fascinating aesthetic history is wrapped up in Strauss's remark.

The orchestras for Richard Strauss's operas are massive; it takes 110 musicians to play *Elektra* and *Der Rosenkavalier* as written, though it is often played with under ninety these days—still a very large opera orchestra. Orchestras grew constantly in the century that separated Beethoven (1770–1827) from Mahler (1860–1911), and by the late nineteenth century large orchestras were the norm. In addition to orchestral size, many of the instruments themselves grew enormously, both in their available range and in volume. Brass instruments, for example, in the time of Beethoven and Mozart, were much smaller than they became over the nineteenth century. And as they grew larger, they also became considerably louder, which meant the string sections had to grow to balance. Wagner, a revolutionary on every level, created orchestral textures and combinations of instruments no one had ever heard before, even inventing or revising brass instruments to make the sounds he wanted.

Wagner tubas, for example, are not actually tubas but revised French horns, played by hornists and capitalizing on the unique requirements of the most difficult of instruments to play. French horns in the eighteenth century and early part of the nineteenth were played with various lengths of tubing called "crooks," which had to be changed depending on the larger-scale key of whatever piece was being played, for crooked horns can only play notes based on the overtone series, one of the self-proving scientific axioms of music. Horns were pitched in G, F, E, E-flat, C, B-flat, A, and D, sometimes all in one work, which meant every time a key changed, the horn player had to alter the hardware, find the crook that corresponded to the length of tubing they would need to play in that key, insert it into the horn, and play. The valve horn was developed to address these complications and to allow horns to play non-chord tones without having to resort to the earlier technique, which was for the horn player to stuff his or her fist into the end of the instrument to diminish the amount of escaping air enough to alter the pitch by a half or whole step.

Flutes of the eighteenth century were made of wood and

had famously unreliable pitch, which may explain why there were so few virtuosi of the flute at the time, but the ones that existed, such as the German flutist Johann Joachim Quantz (1697–1773), were greatly admired for their mastery of this demanding instrument. Flutes appeared rarely in operas of the era; when they did, they generally depicted birds. On the concert stage, though, Telemann, Bach, and Handel wrote a wealth of traverso repertoire, all of it challenging to gifted players right up to this day. One of the most fascinating musical treatises is Quantz's *On Playing the Flute*. Quantz identified the problems inherent in his instrument and found creative ways to improve its performance, adding interlocking keys to what would eventually become the modern fifteen- or sixteen-key flute that was perfected by Theobald Boehm in the mid-nineteenth century. More fascinating than Quantz's thoughts on his chosen instrument, however, valuable as they are, are his beautifully articulated observations of how music was performed in his day, the high baroque; his book is indispensable to the study of baroque performance.

As the nineteenth century progressed, orchestras became larger, and the Beethoven revolution made music more and more complex and difficult to play. Beethoven's nine symphonies, every one of which should be recognizable to any student of the humanities, had musical complexities that could scarcely be comprehended at the time. As orchestras grew larger and music more complex (and we are moving at lightning speed through music history here), the conductor moved from being a practical necessity to being absolutely integral. By the time we arrive at Wagner's mature operas and Mahler's symphonies a short generation later, along with Strauss's own complex music, his dictum to conductors makes a great deal more sense: just because the music got larger doesn't mean the enabling style of the conductor should imitate that size. Keep the beat controlled and clear, the way one must do with Mendelssohn, and don't choreograph the vast sonic gestures of *Salome* and *Elektra*, or any of the larger pieces—just be precise and let the audience hear them.

The growth of the orchestra in size and volume was not happenstance. It was concomitant with huge societal changes reflected in the burgeoning needs for artistic expression throughout the Industrial Revolution: everything got bigger during the late nineteenth century. Musical expression in the Enlightenment can best be understood by drawing parallels with architecture: there was an Enlightenment desire for balance between intellect and emotion and for buildings to be both useful and beautiful. The aesthetic philosophies of the Enlightenment strove for idealism over realism, an aspiration. As the late Romantic era reached its apogee, late in the nineteenth century, both music and architecture clung to a different balance: gargantuan size that would put human size into perspective—a Mahler symphony can easily be heard in the imagination when reflecting on one of the massive buildings of the Austro-Hungarian Empire that still line the Ringstraße or the Eiffel Tower. Surely even now, when we view a more recent creation, such as the Sydney Opera House or the Golden Gate Bridge (both highly derided as they were being built, by the way), we derive some measure of aesthetic pleasure from them because they reflect some aspect of ourselves. That musical works do this is no surprise, but the short century that separates the Enlightenment from the late Romantic era—from, for example, Mozart's 1786 opera *The Marriage of Figaro* to the 1876 premiere of Wagner's seventeen-hour *Der Ring des Nibelungen*—so changed the performance of music in so brief a time that the entire careers of musicians like me are spent learning how that happened. It is an absolutely bottomless and completely fascinating treasure trove, never to be completely discovered.

As much as I admire Richard Strauss's dictums for conductors, I'm much drawn to Pierre Monteux's, for they have a good deal more practical use, and the art of conducting is improved by each of them. I'll name just a few, not in his order:

"Never bend, even for a pianissimo. The effect is too obvious behind." This is true, especially for opera, when so many players are watching you in profile, and when singers on stage cannot hear the orchestra at all, particularly in large Mozart or Rossini ensembles, making them completely dependent on the visual beat.

"Never conduct *for* the audience." Here is a Monteux dictum almost entirely ignored today. I would take it a partial step farther: not only does the conductor not conduct for the audience, but also, he or she isn't there primarily for the orchestra, either: a conductor is present solely as the arbiter of the *score*. A fine conductor should conduct music, not musicians. This doesn't mean a conductor ignores the needs of musicians—far from it—but the primary focus should be enabling them to unlock the score itself, leading us to one of Monteux's great statements.

"Don't be disrespectful to your players (no swearing); don't forget individuals' rights as persons; don't undervalue the members of the orchestra simply because they are 'cogs' in the 'wheels.'"

Further to this, I love Monteux's demand not to "conduct solo instruments in solo passages; don't worry or annoy sections or players by looking intently at them in ticklish passages."

"Don't forget to cue players or sections that have had long

rests, even though the part is seemingly an unimportant inner voice." A conductor must have such a command of the score that he or she is hyper-aware of these long rests, particularly in very complicated operas. The exchange of energy between a knowing and sensitive conductor and a section that has been counting is one of the most vital to the conductor-orchestra relationship, which brings me to two wonderful final Monteux instructions: "Don't come before the orchestra if you have not mastered the score; don't practice or learn the score 'on the orchestra,'" and "Don't stop for obviously accidental wrong notes." Young conductors break these last two all the time, as they are an inevitable part of learning to conduct. "Knowing a score" means, essentially, having it memorized. All conductors know the feeling of knowing something only on the surface, or having fear intervene into one's knowledge. You can never be prepared enough. By the time I conducted *Tristan und Isolde* for the first time, I had been studying the score for thirty years, yet performing it in real time so terrified me that I felt for many days that I didn't know it at all. It forced me to go deeper into the *Ring* operas, and that was what released me from that feeling. No doubt when and if I have the opportunity to return to *Tristan und Isolde* as a more experienced conductor, the feeling will be different.

The greatest writing on conducting, though, is by Richard Wagner. Wagner's many polemical political writings, much of which are rather nonsensical, and his disgraceful anti-Semitic rantings are all best left to the dustbin of history. But get the man to talk about conducting, and his ideas have a cogency that makes one feel as if they were written yesterday. Wagner thought that the principal task of a conductor was not interpretation (though he was by all reports a highly original interpreter himself) but simply to find the composer's tempo. Wagner created the cult of the conductor, yet, as with so much about him, he theorized a desire for its opposite: a conductor who would sublimate his own personality to that of the score itself. Wagner remembers hearing unconducted orchestral performances in his youth and comments, "At least there was no 'disturbing individuality' in the shape of a conductor!"

Footnote: I say "his" because Wagner would likely not have been able to conceive of a female conductor. Happily, things have changed considerably, so that one hears less about "female conductors" and more simply about "conductors," some of whom happen to be male and some female. There are still great strides to be made, to be sure, but the profession has definitely opened up to more diversity than would have been thought possible in Wagner's day.

Wagner's book *On Conducting* contains its fair bit of non-sense as well: the usual rants about non-Germans and questions concerning the abilities of everyone he has ever encountered. But he also directly addresses, in very plain language, issues that perennially face orchestral execution: playing ascending passages without unwritten accents, smooth string crossings, and, most vehemently, conductors who consistently fail to find the right tempi because they are ignorant of singing. His entire thesis can be completely summed up in a single paragraph, one that contains more truth about conducting than many entire books on the subject:

> The whole duty of a conductor is comprised in his ability
> always to indicate the right *tempo*. His choice of tempi will
> show whether he understands the piece or not. With good
> players again the true tempo induces correct phrasing and
> expression, and conversely, with a conductor, the idea of

appropriate phrasing and expression will induce the conception of the true tempo.

He is most relevant in speaking of Bach's music, for Bach doesn't indicate tempo at all, a point that led to Wagner's own decision later in his life not to indicate precise tempi. He rails against "quadrupeds," conductors who insist on conducting four beats to the bar when the music is best executed in two. I have found this to be uniquely true in Wagner: passages that in study I was absolutely certain should be executed in four were invariably improved in some larger beat, either two or one to the bar. This is unique to Wagner's music. He conceived music in such a way as to make its execution unquestionable, something I've experienced with very few composers— perhaps only late Verdi, which simply requires that you do what the man wrote; it needs nothing else.

The conducting student must wade through a small amount of Wagner's usual nasty nationalism and even an anti-Semitic dig near the end of his essay on conducting, but having waded, this is perhaps the most vital piece of writing on conducting that exists. It is typical of Wagner that we must put up with not only his intemperance but his scandalous life. This was, after all, a man who had no compunction about taking others people's money and other people's wives and using them solely to his own benefit, a man who built a theater dedicated solely to his own creations, not even allowing an occasional Mozart or Beethoven opera or one of Richard Strauss's denser works. Wagner accepted the patronage and affection of a homosexual king, even as he openly abhorred homosexuals, apparently seeing no problem in the duplicity. He also railed against Jewish musicians who had actively enabled his career, such as Giacomo Meyerbeer and Hans von Bülow, who were so generous to the man and were repaid with hatred. He didn't attend the funeral of his first wife, despite their thirty-year marriage. Some have disgracefully tried to excuse or defuse Wagner's anti-Semitism by saying it was simply "of its time," or that "everyone was anti-Semitic in those days," but even given the tenor of the times, Wagner's views were abhorrent.

But there was another Wagner, too, and it is this Wagner who inspires and feeds the intellect and the heart, and will continue to do so for as long as thinking people seek him out. This is the Wagner who composed the luscious *Wesendonck Lieder* and who spent nearly three decades writing the *Ring*, one of the profoundest works of art ever created. There is Wagner the librettist and poet, whose libretti alone stand at the peak of achievement in the field, meaning that he would be a cultural landmark even if he had not written a note of music. There is the Wagner who ignited a cultural fire that is still burning, who demanded more of artists than had ever before been demanded, whose questions about the role of art in society we are still trying to answer. It must give us hope, purely as humans, that such a complicated and largely deplorable man could author some of the most life-affirming and brilliant works of art in history. Wagner is one of the great contradictory miracles of history, and perhaps the most human: we long for creative artists to be nobler than the rest of us, but with Wagner that can't be true. That he was so brilliant humanizes us all in that his art is aspirational and his life a lesson in what to avoid. As he said so beautifully, "Art exists as the pure expression of a free community's joy in itself."

From Heavenly Harmony

Inexplicable things constantly happen to me in London. Several years ago I made an early-morning visit to Westminster Abbey, that great reliquary of British history, to seek out the gravesite of my favorite composer, George Frideric Handel. I found the great Abbey uncharacteristically silent, a rare state for so popular a destination. I found Handel's grave peacefully ensconced amidst the fitting company of Shakespeare, Longfellow, and Tennyson, and I sat quietly in the ancient coolness of Poet's Corner.

After a good deal of time contemplating the man, I heard distant music. With the Abbey's busy schedule of musical performances, I assumed it was a rehearsal for some upcoming service. As I moved toward the exit, the music became clearer; it was Handel's *Ode for Saint Cecilia's Day*. Definitely a rehearsal, I thought. The Abbey is so huge that it didn't surprise me not to actually see any musicians. I sat down to listen to that extraordinary work, ruminating on how elegantly the ancient and the modern can coexist.

Opera often dwells in the past. Over the last fifty years, the "authenticity" movement has taught us innumerable lessons about Handel, who, despite a prodigious output, was known for too long on the basis of only one work, his sublime *Messiah*. Audiences of Handel's day had an insatiable appetite for new music; indeed, there was little else performed at the time. Because Handel often conducted his own works, he could easily communicate his intentions directly to the performers; it is not surprising, therefore, that a type of musical shorthand developed between composer and performer, something early-music performers still work to unlock.

Long before our cultural enslavement to photographic realism, and even longer before the marketing of "authentic" (the word must be taken with suspicion) performance practice, there was a dazzling era of operatic performance that prized spontaneity over predictability—an era that valued and sought improvised expressivity, where opera stars aspired to instrumental virtuosity and also the converse: the orchestra's ability to imitate vocal sound was paramount. The baroque era produced an absolutely vast repertoire, much of it lost and even most of the extant pieces unperformed since, and the jewel in the crown of that era was the German-born, Italian-trained, and London-working George Frideric Handel (1685–1759). We are still in the midst of a post-Mahlerian mania for performance-practice "authenticity," an inevitable splintering of approaches that is the result of little public interest in newly composed music, which forces a focus on varied approaches to the music of the past. In the early days of the "authentic instrument" movement, the focus was very much on playing music exactly as a composer heard it, on researching musical texts that were free of orchestral embellishments and enlargements. Now, thankfully, the emphasis has moved to using what we've learned to create thrilling in-the-moment experiences for audiences that simultaneously embrace authenticity, acknowledging that historical authenticity and contemporary thrills are utterly compatible, something that would not have been a given when my career started in the mid-1980s.

The fundamental purpose of vocal ornamentation is to heighten the expression or spiritual potency of the text. Any given ornament should serve the words and not simply be an empty display of virtuosity. Handel's extraordinary arias are miniature inner monologues, textually sparse and repetitious, but musically—and thus, emotionally—continuous. The singers—or, more precisely, the characters the singers are portraying—improvise notes around those the composer Handel wrote ("riffing," as it's called in jazz). Sometimes these improvisations are planned in advance, but more often they are spontaneous. These embellishments heighten the various emotional states of a character and give the listener various views of an emotion; think of vocal ornaments as a sort of musical camera angle. The thrill of Handel's operas comes from how astoundingly modern they feel, how clean and honest. Handel's slower arias fall on the ear as silk falls on the skin, sensuous and liquid, but he can also summon extraordinary amounts of musical energy and send a character into dazzling heights of fury or exaltation. And perhaps the most extraordinary aspect of Handel's operas is how much room he leaves in them for the personality of a performer; for as great as the works are on the page, it is only through live performance, through the imagination of improvised invention, that they can be truly heard. The Handelian renaissance of the past few decades has revealed one of opera's great musical dramatists, a true man of the theater, unquestionably on the level of Mozart, Verdi, and Wagner.

It is thanks to the pioneers of the authenticity movement that we can now be confident in interpreting not only what Handel did write down but also, what is more important, the inferences of what he did not. For example, certain rhythmically "even," repeated figures should be played unevenly. Some, but not all, types of dotted figures should be double-dotted, creating a very angular rhythmic pattern. "Tempo" markings in the baroque era indicate mood more often than speed. Certain types of emotional situations lend themselves to ornamentation, others less so. We have learned about the size of Handel's orchestras, although modern performances must take into account theaters that are huge by comparison to those in which Handel was heard during his lifetime. We have learned that the dynamic range of Handel's day was not as polarized as ours today. Knowledge of baroque instruments also informs our musical interpretation. We have gained profound insights into baroque bowing style in string instruments: rather than trying to impose a modern, "continuous melody" bow stroke, a shorter, elegant stroke more aptly supports Handel's long melodic structure and his sequences of tension and release (baroque bows were of much lighter weight and differently balanced than their modern equivalents). The list of "authenticity" discoveries is endless.

Despite the positive effect of the authenticity movement on the way we perform Handel, one dilemma remains: we cannot hope to recreate the expectations and the experiences of an audience that is hearing Handel's operas as contemporary music. Eighteenth-century audiences did not sit politely in a darkened theater: the house lights (candles) remained illumined throughout the performance to facilitate glances at the translated Italian libretto. Eating, drinking, and talking were rampant (though I wonder if even an eighteenth-century public could have tolerated cellular phones), and one does not even want to contemplate the restroom break of eighteenth-century London. The private boxes were home to an abundant array of assignations, from commercial dealings to some slightly older pleasures. So it is important that we honor Handel not by imprisoning him with immutable dogma, but by utilizing our knowledge of his time to create something new and relevant in the context of the modern opera house. By giving contemporary audiences an opportunity to hear Handel's music with their own ears and expectations, the ancient informs the modern.

On the surface, Handel's music falls elegantly upon the ear, but a deeper exploration of his London masterpieces, particularly *Rodelinda*, *Agrippina*, *Serse* (Xerxes), *Ariodante*, and *Giulio Cesare* (Julius Caesar), reveals a complex and profoundly dramatic composer whose music can change stock characters into figures of Shakespearean depth, even while ravishing the ear with dazzling bravura and melodic invention. Handel's writing for the human voice is extraordinary, surpassed only by that of Mozart (who admired and emulated Handel, going so far as to reorchestrate Handel's *Messiah* and *Acis and Galatea*—an act of homage, not hubris). Each character is presented in a boundless variety of vocal and orchestral writing. Caesar and Cleopatra naturally have the majority of the tours de force, but the secondary characters all have their characteristically diverse showpieces. Cleopatra's many arias illuminate a fascinating woman, from her erotic "V'adoro pupille" to the heartrending "Se pietà di me non senti" and "Piangerò la sorte mia." Handel's Italian operas have none of the vast fugal choruses one hears in his great English oratorios. Characters so rarely sing together that it is particularly effective when they do: Cornelia and Sextus, mother and son, have one of the most poignantly tragic duets in all opera.

The castrati, adult male singers surgically altered in their youth to preserve their treble ranges, were the great stars of Handel's era; enraptured audiences did not shout "Bravo!" to the castrati, but rather "Evviva il coltello!" (Hail to the knife!). They are honored today by an elite group of distinguished countertenors, in numbers unthinkable even a quarter of a century ago, who have reached their rare vocal status through more pleasantly organic means than did their predecessors. Handel was clearly inspired by the virtuosity of the great castrati Senesino and Farinelli, with the most poignant and demanding music in *Giulio Cesare* going to the countertenors. Listen for the achingly sad beauty of Caesar's "Aure, deh, per pietà," and how vividly it contrasts with his joyously humorous duet with the solo violin "Se in fiorito ameno prato." Caesar's aria "Va tacito e nascosto" presents the first use of the solo French horn in opera and remains, nearly three centuries later, an exemplar of brilliant writing for the instrument. The audiences of Handel's day were not likely to have a judgment about the masculinity of a male character singing in a female register: high pitch simply symbolized high rank. If there is an obstacle for modern audiences in appreciating a baroque opera, it tends to be the organization of the narrative, the plot. Unlike later popular operas, such as *La traviata* or *Tosca*, which attempted to portray realistic situations, baroque operas purposefully evaded reality; allegory was considered the most direct route to emotional clarity. Some criticize baroque arias for "stopping the action," perhaps not realizing that they are designed to do so. Handel's arias are a matrix through which emotion is dissected and experienced. For maximum enjoyment, surrender your investment in psychological reality and allow yourself to experience a vast tapestry of emotion and intellect. Handel evokes more than he portrays, so don't let yourself spend the evening glued to the supertitles; he dwells most often in the more subtle sphere beyond words, in the realm of the spirit. Baroque music correlates to that moment of possibility presented in the bouquet of newly opened wine, not the feeling you have once the bottle has been emptied.

I often think back to that early morning in Westminster Abbey and wonder if I actually did hear an organ and a choir. In the passing years I find myself choosing to ignore the most logical explanation, preferring instead to imagine something more mystical, as though Handel's music might always be there lying in wait to be heard and I just happened to tune in at the right moment, like some cosmic radio. I recall the choir finishing John Dryden's great words, "From harmony, from heavenly harmony this universal frame began," just before I found myself back out in modern London, hailing a cab.

Conducting a Life

What of my own experience of conducting? I can speak only for myself, of course, as all conductors are different and, for obvious reasons, we rarely work together. I was so fortunate to have Charles Mackerras and André Previn in my early career as mentors and friends. Charles, in particular, had the most musical influence on me, though he never talked about the physicalization of music, about gesture. It wasn't important to him. What mattered to him was the science of music, the intellectual semantics, because he felt that if a conductor got those right, the audience would have access to the most important elements of music. The spiritual qualities of music would have been completely irrelevant to him because he couldn't possibly have imagined a conductor even worrying about that. For him, it was our job to make the music available at its highest level.

André loves and believes in music more than anyone I've ever known. There is no end to his fascination with the works he loves, and the breadth of his tastes is vast. He would comment on gesture, not to make anyone conduct the way he did, but to ensure that your idea came naturally out of the arm.

Conducting is challenging because no one is ever good at all of it. I've been better at some times in life than others, and by far the greatest struggle I have had as a performer has been presence, in every sense of the word. A conductor must be willing to be known, and I have closed off that ability on many occasions, usually out of simple fear, or from some unplanned distraction. The greatest conductors allow no distractions, and I'm more able to be undistracted as I age. In my younger days, I was distracted by everything, and fear is the largest distraction of all. When one is a young person in an older person's profession, it is enormously difficult to face an orchestra of older peers and feel you have something worth saying. And conducting is an art in which much of what one has to say is best left unsaid; it must be emanated without words. You are judged and summed up within minutes, and it is difficult to ever change those impressions, particularly in very busy ensembles that are under constant pressure to perform and have little interest in introspection.

The "fame" part of the profession has little to do with the art itself, and that is blindsiding. Fame is, obviously, only about what you have been perceived to achieve, so that is all in the past. It has nothing to do with what true artists focus upon, which is what is happening in the future. It is true that fame and reputation are what keep you working, but they can also hinder you from working when they become the motivating factor of a career. It is ultimately only the music itself and one's relationship to it that never disappoints; while the career lets one down constantly unless one's motivations are securely focused.

I've been best at conducting when I felt both secure and supported (rare), when I was with colleagues I admired to the core (joyfully often), and when I was conducting a work I absolutely loved (almost always). The combination of the three is complete magic. I observe in colleagues whom I most admire that they are able to have fulfilling experiences no matter how secure they feel and no matter whether they get along with their colleagues, and I admire that focus and wish I had it. Considering the variety of works I've performed, I've had surprisingly few experiences that I consider compromised to the point of feeling like a failure, many that sit in a middle ground of fulfilling memories, and a few were experiences of such beauty that even a moment's reflection upon them brings tears. I had several early occasions when I indulged singers too much, naively thinking that to be my job.

A surprisingly large number of my most fulfilling memories involve Handel repertoire: *Rodelinda* at the Metropolitan Opera, *Serse* and *Ariodante* at San Francisco Opera, *Rinaldo* at Opera Australia, and *Giulio Cesare* in Houston and, many years ago, at Wolf Trap, in the halcyon summer of 1995. These were forever times, endlessly special to me, particularly *Serse*, as I think it was the most joyous time I've ever spent as a conductor and the finest work I've done to date. I can't pretend to know why or what others feel after conducting Handel, but I know that I feel a different and cleansed energy at the conclusion of what feels to *me* like a great Handel performance, whether or not I'm conducting. This is a feeling that is, for me, unique to Handel. Gluck's *Iphigénie en Tauride*, one of my very favorite operas, in San Francisco and at the Metropolitan Opera, remains a time of real presence, both remembered by me as if they were yesterday. Jake Heggie's major world premieres, all of which I have conducted, carry similar feelings, for they were impactful and challenging operas peopled with colleagues I adored. No one present at the opening night of *Dead Man Walking* in San Francisco will ever forget it, for it was suddenly a new era, and we were then the upstart kids who had been handed a project to which most people gave no credence—until it went well. Other experiences stand in relief in my memory: *Werther, Falstaff, Lucia di Lammermoor, Lohengrin, Billy Budd,* countless performances of *La traviata* and *The Marriage of Figaro,* and *The Maids,* by Peter Bengston, in Cincinnati, an incredibly profound modern masterpiece.

And then, unsurprisingly, the Wagner *Ring* in Houston, spread over four seasons, 2014–17, an enormous milestone for a company that had never before performed it. A little bit of context is required to understand the magnitude of this achievement: David Gockley, the longtime general director of Houston Grand Opera who left in 2005 to helm the San Francisco Opera, had concluded officially to the HGO board that "this is not a *Ring* company" after he and I had explored the possibility of doing the Zurich production of the cycle (by Robert Wilson, which I loved) in the early 2000s. In truth, the orchestra wasn't ready at that time, and in deeper truth, David simply didn't have any interest in it at that point in his career. Just as David's replacement, Anthony Freud, left HGO after six years to head the Lyric Opera of Chicago, and when Perryn Leech and I were asked to jointly step into the general director role, HGO was engaged in a verbal agreement with Opera Australia for a *Ring* production with a producer I deeply admire, Neil Armfield, and with whom I'd had some of my favorite experiences. Neil is a theatrical genius and a director capable of creating that rarest rehearsal environment of creativity and inclusivity. His rehearsals are bliss.

In my first six weeks as artistic director, we held a design presentation of the first two *Ring* operas, *Das Rheingold* and *Die Walküre*, and despite my admiration and respect for Neil, I simply didn't like the results, and it didn't feel to me like a cycle that would sustain interest over four years and garner the type of extraordinary support that the work would to be generate. Ultimately, an artistic director has to be able to speak with authentic passion about every project the company produces, since fund-raising is simply a sharing of passion. I knew that with the best will in the world I would never be able to do that with the Opera Australia *Ring*, and I regretfully but resolutely removed HGO from the agreement.

Perryn, as managing director, quite rightly said to me, "well, what *Ring are* we doing now that we aren't working with Australia?" An artistic director then has a number of choices to make. Do we rent an existing production? Do we recreate a famous production? Do we develop our own completely new production? The last option is the most artistically satisfying, but it is also the most time-consuming and expensive. To develop a new production of the four operas would have required approximately another decade when one includes the time of selecting a director and design team, developing the productions, presenting them, approving them, costing them, building them—and then four years to rehearse and perform them. And I knew I didn't want to delay.

Having seen nearly every *Ring* in the world over the previous twenty years, I kept thinking back to the experience of seeing the cycle in Valencia, Spain, in the dazzling new opera house designed by Santiago Calatrava. I had seen the cycle there produced by La Fura dels Baus, a Catalan theatrical group that had done very little opera up to that point. This was as far from a conventional *Ring* as one could imagine, yet the production had extraordinary narrative clarity about it; one would have to willfully misunderstand the visual imagery, or simply be a curmudgeon, not to at least accord it respect, regardless of whether one "liked" it. Exploring the idea further, I found the fascinating reason that the Fura dels Baus *Ring* had such a combination of clarity and theatrical whizz-bangery: Carlus Padrissa, the Cherubino-like director of the production, had never seen a production of the *Ring* before directing and ushering in the designs of this cycle. What he did was return to the Eddas and Norse literature that inspired Wagner. He spent month after month studying the text of the *Ring* and listening to the music. He did not, as so many directors do, react against something that had been done before in another production, and I loved this quality in particular.

What he created was as *gesamt*, as complete, a production as has been produced in a generation, and it inspired the Houston audience as nothing in our history has ever done, on a par with the 1976 *Porgy and Bess* that put the company on the operatic map in the first place. The theatrical thrills did not diminish the work of a largely new Wagnerian generation, headed by Christine Goerke and Iain Paterson as Brünnhilde and Wotan, and so many others, many of whom were outside the traditional opinion culture of our peer companies when we cast them.

It would take another book to talk about each of my own highlights of conducting the cycle: the titanic feeling of the final minute of *Das Rheingold*, an opera that begins and ends with watery imagery; the "I can't believe I'm seeing this" quality of the of human exoskeleton of Valhalla, conjuring the human toil of the great palace; the human eggs Alberich is harvesting in Nibelheim, placing human life at the center of the interpretation; the unearthly vibration of conducting the end of *Siegfried*, which is my favorite of the operas. I think it best to illustrate just one brief moment.

When one reaches the end of *Götterdämmerung*, it is common to assume that the conductor is physically tired. This wasn't true for me. I was wistful, not wanting it to end. And I was energized, my mind continuing to blaze for another five hours after the last chord. These are works that change the color of one's soul, and there is no other way to describe it. Is this not a spiritual feeling, the feeling of personal transformation, of not being the same person at 11:20 P.M. that one was when we started at 6:00 P.M.? The spiritual feeling is not that of accomplishment. Many people have conducted and played the *Ring*, and it is true that it takes a lifetime of study and preparation to do it well; but it isn't what one feels, or it wasn't what I felt. I felt a kinship with something larger than my own thoughts.

Our Contribution to the Human Spirit

"I am certain that after the dust of centuries has passed
over our cities, we, too, will be remembered not for our
victories or defeats in battle or in politics, but for our
contribution to the human spirit."
—**John F. Kennedy**, at a closed-circuit television
broadcast on behalf of the National Cultural Center,
November 29, 1962

The experience of conducting is ultimately too large to ar-
ticulate, but perhaps sharing one microcosm might help: the
Funeral March of Siegfried, which ends the second scene of
Götterdämmerung's third act, for it is significantly more than
what it is known to be, a musical tour of Siegfried's life. In its
short duration, especially by Wagnerian standards, it depicts
the very idea of hero. It feels like a farewell not solely to a fic-
tional character, but to an entire era. It is emotionally and

intellectually moving on every level: musical, theatrical, and philosophical, an elegy not only to the dead hero but to the whole idea of heroism. We have, through the long hours of the *Ring*, spent a great deal of time with Siegfried. We know him, and so his death affects us personally if we have been engaged with the drama. Siegfried is the epochal hero, the reason that Wagner engaged his gigantic intellect in the cycle in the first place. He thought that his era, especially by the late 1840s, was in need of historic national heroes. Germanic characters, he believed, had weakened through his lifetime, and he wanted to return art to its connections to the epic and historic. Of course, Wagner being Wagner, he not only wrote a historic character in Siegfried, but he did so by writing one of the largest works of art ever conceived to explain him. The character of Siegfried is, as often noted by commentators, Wagner himself, the hero who knows no fear, a character raised by a man not his father, a man destined to save the world (artistically at least, in Wagner's case) only to be killed (metaphorically at least, in Wagner's case) by those who didn't understand his importance.

Wagner's art became his life, not such an unusual thing for an artist; but Wagner's art was, and still is, more intense, more profound, and more demanding than most. What does "profundity" mean in this case? Any art is dependent on the depth of the person experiencing it. A profound opera such as *Tristan und Isolde* displays, for example, endless layers of meaning, and it does so differently at different stages of one's life. I've often felt there to be secrets within *Tristan und Isolde* that I didn't want to know, a fact that has troubled me in trying to prepare and conduct the work. I had to remain at an emotional remove from it for a long time, too long to be truly present within it, but I'm sure that will change when I approach the work again later in life. It is true that for some, *Tristan und Isolde* is nothing more than a dark and glacial love story with a transcendent ending; for me it was like staring into oblivion itself, and it terrified me.

Götterdämmerung, although the longest opera of the *Ring*, is also the most conventional in most respects. It has a lot of traditional operatic elements that wouldn't be out of place in French or Italian operas (potions, trios, choruses, oaths, betrayals), but it has so much more besides: the psychological embedding of motives in *Götterdämmerung* is so complex that even after a lifetime of study or appreciation one will still discover new ideas in its dense score.

Near the middle of the third act comes the culminating point of the entire cycle, the Funeral March of Siegfried, who has been killed by Hagen. Brünnhilde, the great warrior princess whom Siegfried conquered, had protected everything except Siegfried's back, believing it pointless because he would never turn his back on an enemy.

It is programmatic, descriptive, and poetic music. The musical motives associated with Siegfried are embedded fifteen measures into the very brief passage of the march, which is in total less than 1 percent of *Götterdämmerung*'s score, fewer than sixty measures of music in an opera than contains an astonishing 6,040 measures of music (the conductor of this opera gives over 20,000 individual beats in a single performance).

In my profession, conducting, "fast" is flippant and "slow" is profound, the opposite of cars. This comes particularly into play in Wagner, when the pace of the conductor can greatly affect the length of the evening, not to mention the ability of the singers to deliver the phrases in single discernible sentences. Wagner didn't leave metronome markings for most of his music, in the way Verdi and many others did, but he did leave constant expectations about the length of his works, and the early years of the Bayreuth Festival started a tradition of meticulous timings of the individual Wagner acts. Tempo in Wagner is as much a feeling as it is an actual pace—one can pace it very quickly and it will feel slow, or elongate phrases that one will wish were slightly longer. Wagner tends to create more of himself at every turn.

There is nothing in opera to equal the weight of feeling when conducting Siegfried's Funeral March. It isn't technically difficult to conduct, yet it takes a lifetime of conducting to do it well. It is written in such a way that the conductor must execute several technical feats that, as Wagner knew very well, only a few could pull off. Much of Wagner has this quality: extraordinarily difficult to play but not to conduct. In fact, both *Lucia di Lammermoor* and *La traviata* require a great many more technical decisions and much more skill purely in terms of technique, yet it is rarely the conductor one remembers at the ends of those operas. It is music that is conceived for conducting; but isn't all orchestral music from about 1850 onward so conceived?

Parsifal and *Tannhäuser* are two opposite sides of Wagner's psyche. *Tannhäuser* is an overtly Christian pilgrimage story that is written, even with Wagner's staggeringly beautiful score, wholly in the French grand opera style. *Parsifal*, though, is something else entirely, the true music of the future, much more so than *Tristan und Isolde*. *Parsifal* has yet to be fully understood, for it contains many dense (some might say impenetrable) ideas gathered from the world's spiritual traditions as Wagner understood them at the time. No production of *Parsifal* can be considered a definitive reading of it because so many of its ideas are purposefully left foggy by Wagner, awaiting a future generation of interpreters to illuminate it. Was this deliberate on Wagner's part, or was he the muse, through the composition of *Parsifal*, of some larger idea? There is the surface plot of the opera, which is ostensibly an Arthurian epic about the Holy Grail; but then there are the layers of meaning below that surface, and this is where *Parsifal* assumes its role as a spiritual force, one the world is ever more in need of. If this seems an extraordinary claim, try to describe the *Parsifal*'s spiritual power without just one of its elements. It is a unified totality with text entirely dependent on music and vice versa, and with production entirely dependent on score and vice versa. One could make this claim about any opera, but not to the degree with which it is true of *Parsifal*, the most spiritual work ever conceived for the operatic stage. It is unlikely to ever be equaled, but I hope composers will continue to try.

It Goes On

Opera carries within its history a concurrent and recognizable musical history that has always informed its conventions. Yet operas conveyed in the polyglot musical languages of the twenty-first century have a great deal of trouble finding a large enough public to become part of the active repertoire, at least as we have always defined it in the past. But the cultural benchmarks have shifted in our technological information age, in which nearly everything is available with a click. Concurrently, we are in an era that possesses a dizzying level of compositional mastery of classical music, yet we also feel culturally, as if we are at the end of something: the burgeoning growth and expectation of constant expansion of arts institutions that was assumed and achieved in the post–World War II era is no longer a common feeling among artists. Compositionally, the European modernism that descended from the Second Viennese School became the permanent touchstone and lodestar of all classical compositions to nearly all students of music and certainly to the majority of major music critics, and anything that deviated from that path was considered regressive, no matter how successful it was with the public. Logically, this limited the musical possibilities of classical music, particularly opera, which by its nature is a deeper and more expensive commitment of time and resource, and relegated it to a largely intellectual pursuit.

The current business of the arts in the United States can't be said to be especially vibrant, but the art itself has never been more filled with possibilities and gifted artisans. Oxymoron? Newspapers are not news, nor are history books history, artistic organizations are not art. They are the guides, custodians, visionaries, and, hopefully, the builders of the art, but they aren't the art itself—a feeling that is growing ever more acute in arts organizations around the world, many of whom are scrambling to adjust their activities to the rapid cultural changes of the age. Interest in artistic pursuits and great storytelling has not diminished, yet traditional attendance and adherence to the past, and trying to hold to the tenets of a theory, are certainly endangered.

It has now been ninety years since an opera has permanently entered the repertoire; that was Puccini's *Turandot*. In contemplating the phenomenal success of Puccini's operas from our vantage point, there are some important things to remember. He was a great absorbent creator, melding all sorts of compositional and theatrical traditions within his operas while retaining his own voice. And while many of his operas are now loved by the public, they weren't immediately so, and they have never been critically acclaimed even if performances of them have been.

The pace of operatic creativity slowed considerably af-

ter Puccini because of the two world wars and the global economic depression between them that, all combined, occupied
a third of the last century. By the end of World War II, the
lines of compositional creativity had been permanently sev-
ered. This is the reason that the list of post-*Turandot* operas
that have found a place, however tenuous, in the repertoire
is so brief—just nine operas in sixty years, and even this list
has an arguably tenuous claim on being part of the active repertoire: *Porgy and Bess*, *Peter Grimes*, *Amahl and the Night
Visitors*, *The Ballad of Baby Doe*, *Susannah*, *The Crucible*,
Dialogues of the Carmelites, *Vanessa*, and *Nixon in China*.
This is not to say that there haven't been many other noble
efforts and many wonderful works written in that time; this
is simply a statement of the fact of the annual repertoire, as
much as we would like it to be otherwise.

But the tide is turning, and we are on the cusp of something new and uniquely American in its assimilation. I believe that all culture in the twenty-first century, particularly
opera, is rather rapidly evolving in a new era of creative fusion, a melding of many disciplines and traditions into new
forms. There is, to my mind, sufficient evidence that opera is
reinventing itself, though it isn't always doing so in the traditional ways in traditional opera houses. And one doesn't read
a great deal about it, because there are fewer avenues in which
to do so, and for most U.S. arts companies, getting read about
simply means being mentioned in the *New York Times*.

The *New York Times*, though, at least in matters operatic,
is ubiquitously Eurocentric, despite having the finest team of
writers on the arts of any publication in the world. Indeed,
one could never tell from reading the *New York Times* that the
opera companies of Santa Fe and Houston have presented annual operatic commissions on a variety of scales (sometimes

more than one) for fifty or forty years, respectively, nor that San Francisco, Minnesota, Chicago, Dallas, Los Angeles, Washington, and other companies have commissioned far more ambitiously and regularly than the only American opera company on which the *Times* regularly reports, its hometown company (though it prides itself on being an "international" newspaper in other matters), rightfully respected for reasons other than its contributions to replenishing the repertoire.

We must surely work from a definition of opera as musical storytelling, but on this question there is little consensus: Is opera a single art form, long defined, or is it evolving with fluidity and gathering and fusing with other art forms as it does so? Is the musical language evolving, or does opera utilize existing musical linguistics while focusing on relevant modern topics? Is the evolution of musical language more important than the content of that language? These are not small questions for writers on opera and classical music, and there is so little consensus about opera's definition that it feels as though the questions will exist as long as opera does. I've even read (though thankfully not in the *New York Times*) that if a great opera is written in the future, it will be in a musical language we don't yet recognize. Imagine that aesthetic applied to any other art: a painting can be modern only if it forgoes oils, pastels, watercolors, or acrylics, or, a novel can be great only if it utilizes language in a way never before tried. In other arts this hermeneutic would be thought ludicrous, but applied to modern composers it is common.

Surely all of the accomplished contributors to the *New York Times* and other national publications would admit that opera is, and always has been, an amalgam of many art forms. So it remains today: American opera in recent years has particularly shown its resistance to theory, as the most successful composers with the only people who have a deciding vote in their lasting worth—audiences—have been artistic centrists who have fused the past with their own voices. Music critics are understandably and continually drawn to the (largely) European modernists, and musicians revere them too—that is, after all, what we all learned in conservatory. But audiences have spoken, loudly, consistently, and clearly, for generations, that they will accept the modernists in small doses and in the context of other more, accessible new music.

To most composers of the past, "accessible" was not the horrifying word it is for some now, nor was popularity, prior to the twentieth century, a sign of artistic insignificance. That music critics, even the very finest of them, have been notoriously poor at predicting the lasting power of any serious musical works is well-known, and the finest critics have always acknowledged it. But we are at a particularly crucial impasse between what will be critically respected or maligned and what audiences will respond to and keep in the repertoire.

Many operas written in the past thirty years have been successful with audiences but overlooked by critics. We've had large-scale world premieres in Houston that the *New York Times* and other national press organs have declined to review because they were defined as "of regional interest," and the *Times* considers itself, justifiably, an international newspaper. But it must also be said that the *Times* has managed always to find time and money to cover European cultural activities that were similarly regional, though since the region was Europe, it was deemed worthy.

Is the only available language for opera modernism, itself a term that is now extraordinarily broad? Is there no room to define opera in the very ways audiences define it, as stories told primarily through affecting and emotionally moving music? The critical culture largely has yet to embrace the breadth of activity of much of modern opera of recent years. One rarely hears mention of *Florencia en el Amazonas* by Daniel Catán, an enormous success with audiences everywhere it has played; nor has any critic written deeply on Daniel's utterly singular compositional voice. What of the Pulitzer Prize–winning *Silent Night*, by Kevin Puts, one of the most moving operas of recent years? How often does one read of Mark Adamo's *Little Women*, an American adaptation of an American novel that is utterly unique in the repertoire? Major critics have long eschewed the longest-standing dean of American operatic composers, a major composer continually treated with arrogance by the *New York Times*, Carlisle Floyd. What of Lyric Opera of Chicago's glorious, lyrical, ambitious, and soaring *McTeague* by William Bolcom? Audiences flocked to and cried over Ricky Ian Gordon's *The Grapes of Wrath*, but one would never discern this from the dwindling national musical press. Péter Eötvös wrote an operatic version of Tony Kushner's *Angels in America*, arguably the greatest epic play of our time, and even Kushner acknowledged it as an operatic masterwork; interestingly, it has been largely critically acclaimed as a European opera. Meredith Monk's *Atlas*, premiered in Houston in the 1990s, is sadly forgotten, yet it is a major work surely in need of revival. Two major composers often cited by the *New York Times*, John Adams and Kaija Saariaho, are most often covered for their European commissions, not for works commissioned by U.S. companies, like Houston Grand Opera's *Nixon in China* or the Santa Fe Opera's *Adriana Mater*, surely one of the most important operas of my lifetime.

Whole schools of nonmodernist composition are regularly

overlooked, particularly of operas that have found success with audiences: Oliver Knussen's *Where the Wild Things Are*, Kirke Mechem's *Tartuffe*, Olivier Messiaen's *Saint François d'Assise* (European modernism, of a sort, so it fares somewhat better), Michael Nyman's *The Man Who Mistook His Wife for a Hat*, Anthony Davis's *X: The Life and Times of Malcolm X*. Or, looking further afield from America or Europe, what of Australia's *The Eighth Wonder*, by Alan John and Dennis Watkins, or the glorious *Voss*, by Richard Meale and David Malouf—two marvelous operas that have yet to be seen in the United States?

The *New York Times* isn't the only newspaper at fault, of course, and in most ways the *Times* is the least at fault, because it still has a relatively robust arts section. Most newspapers have not been so fortunate, which makes the responsibility of the *Times* even greater: it remains the national mouthpiece and newspaper of record. Those of us on the front lines largely outside of New York wish they would notice the vibrant work being done around the country.

It is no surprise that the most successful and renowned (with audiences) opera composer of recent years is still undersung by the *New York Times*. Jake Heggie's *Dead Man Walking* and *Moby-Dick*, both maligned by the various writers of the *New York Times*, have both connected deeply with audiences, opening up a possibility for those audiences to accept other challenges. That Heggie writes tonal and accessible music is hardly the most interesting or descriptive element of his formidable talent, though those are the items on which entrenched modernists most closely focus. Is it not more important, in this time of dwindling interest in the classical arts, that a composer who is able to connect with a large public is to be celebrated, cultivated, and encouraged, rather than defined according to a fixed and immovable nineteenth-century paradigm? Opera is an evolving and morphing entity, capable of great vision and breadth, if our discernment and acuity in hearing them steer well clear of myopia.

Surveying the post–World War II operatic world, it was a golden age of performance and attendance, but not of new creations, while simultaneously the commercial theater was teeming with new works that reached a wide public: the post-war American theatrical composers who followed on the great innovations of Kern and Gershwin: Rodgers, Loewe, Loesser, Porter, Weill, Bernstein, Styne, Bock, Kander, and, eventually, Stephen Sondheim wrote a golden age of American musical theater. What we are seeing now is an emerging set of composers who straddle those worlds with enormous ease, and who each defy the easy classification that has for so long been a part of the academic and theoretical. The worlds of commercial theater and opera are slowly starting to converge, and the risk taking, from a compositional standpoint, is unquestionably now in the opera house rather than the Broadway theater, the opposite of what could be said fifty years ago.

Evolution in art, as in science, moves in stages, and we are at the point with opera, particularly in the United States, where newly evolving forms are emerging more quickly than at any stage since the unparalleled group that followed Wagner's *Parsifal*: *Lakmé, Manon, Khovanshchina, Otello, The Queen of Spades, Prince Igor, Cavalleria rusticana, Pagliacci, Werther, Aleko, Manon Lescaut, Hänsel und Gretel, Falstaff, Thaïs, Andrea Chénier, La bohème, Cendrillon, The Tsar's Bride, Tosca, Louise* (by far the most popular opera of its era), *Rusalka, Pelléas et Mélisande, Saul og David, Tiefland, Jenůfa, Madama Butterfly, Salome, The Merry Widow, La vida breve, Ariane et Barbe-bleue, A Village Romeo and Ju-*

liet, *Elektra*, *Erwartung*, *La fanciulla del West*, *Bluebeard's Castle*, *L'heure espagnole*, and, in a fittingly autumnal ending, *Der Rosenkavalier*, written just as the twentieth century's terrible wars were about to begin. I believe the future of serious composition in the world will be in the more diverse forms that break from the traditional Western orchestra and from the bel canto traditions of opera; we are likely to see many new operas with small performing forces and alternative venues, written in a variety of melded styles, and in venues that are not traditional opera houses. There will likely be no end point at which we notice the culmination of this cultural fusion, but I do believe that we are in the middle of forming a new twenty-first-century repertoire, while recognizing that entrance into the repertoire has often taken some time, often up to fifty years. The next composer to engage a broad public is absolutely out there if he or she is not already actively writing and has simply gone unnoticed. Be prepared not to have these composers receive great and immediate acclaim, not matter how at odds that is with the current climate of immediate classification and cynicism. Composition is no different from other disciplines: it takes practice and experience, but the creative fires are out there burning, and they will find their way to us if we are available to them.

One of my favorite operas is one often dismissed by opera's intelligentsia, Puccini's *Turandot*, which has what André Previn described to me as "the [expletive deleted] greatest three opening measures in music!" I love this opera partly because audiences love it so much, but far from finding it as shallow and its characters underwritten as has been the normal view of the opera, I find it very moving and its characters quite profound, not necessarily in what they say but in what Puccini says about them. That the opera was incomplete at

Puccini's death is part of its poignancy and potency, reminding us that opera is perpetually an unfinished enterprise, a continuous but incomplete song. And that it tells us, finally, that love is the final engine of the human spirit is, to me, one of opera's most potent messages and one we cannot hear often enough. The experience of conducting *Turandot* is an overwhelming one, and I am always surprised at how moving I find it in performance. There are moments in each act that I find so touching that I can barely contain my emotions: "Non piangere, Liù," "Ho una casa nell'Honan," and Puccini's last notes, just after the death of Liù, which contain so much of possibility that still lay ahead of him.

Hoffnung

A deep connection to the spiritual enlargement of music has taught me to cherish experiences in life that are small and perfect, little glimpses of beauty that are easy to overlook. Part of the gestation of an artistic life is developing the ability to identify and live in those moments, to recognize their significance with gratitude. We have too often been encouraged to overlook the joyful or to prioritize the banal, when it is the seemingly ordinary that brings us the most comfort. "Random," that wildly overused (and misused) word of the moment, is a convenient way to express the passing of moments that ought to be significant indeed: people greeting each other at airport arrival areas—is there anything on earth more joyful than that? But how seldom we take a few seconds to notice it. What of the thrilling news (who knew?) that Atlantic spiny lobsters migrate in single file, holding onto each other's backsides for navigation, in lines that can reach up to forty miles? Some of my own small and perfect memories include the sight of two distant white cockatoos in the Blue Mountains of Australia, soaring amidst green and blue gum trees as far as the eye could discern; the gorgeously silent and translucent sunsets on the shores of Lake Constance in Bregenz in the hour before our performances began at the festival; the sight of a single sailboat on Lake Michigan in Chicago, nestled in my view for a moment between the bookends of skyscrapers; the tint of burnt-orange light on an early morning walk in Nanjing, China, as I heard from a survivor about the events that happened on the ground on which we were walking at that moment; the quiet snow in Moscow's Red Square last winter when I was there rehearsing; the deep green of the old forests near my childhood home in southern Indiana. It often takes something larger than life to get us to feel life, but it is surely also true that the smallest random things can take on enormous beauty and meaning if we are available to feel them. How I strive for Montaigne's ability to be surprised by what surrounded him every day—not to require fireworks to get my attention, but to be present for the slight flickering of a small candle, and to know and feel that the two share the same qualities as the stuff of stars.

Recently my colleagues at Houston Grand Opera asked me to write something based on the popular *This I Believe* series as a way of sharing some of my thoughts about art. I blanched, considering the exercise too personal and unseemly, and a little like a test, even though I have never held an elected office and never want to. But it ultimately felt churlish, and a little cowardly, to avoid questioning my own beliefs, particularly in a discussion about art's role in spirituality.

Beliefs

The ancient Greeks thought the highest level of intelligence was an ability to balance belief with knowledge, to have the ability to assess without judgment. Knowledge must be assimilated bit by bit, and our short time in earthly consciousness frustratingly limits what can be acquired. Belief, though, is infinite; we can believe nearly anything, and even a cursory glance at the world proves that we do. I have always had the feeling that one's strongest beliefs are best kept in a noble silence, concerned that sharing them might adversely affect them. Knowledge often seems safer terrain.

In my artistic life, I deal all of the time with the idea of "belief," and with the fact that judgments have to be made based on those beliefs, since a great deal about art is subjective. Every artist is also a critic, and hopefully a temperate one, particularly as we turn our critical eye most often inward.

Beliefs without knowledge are delusions, while knowledge

without beliefs seems pedantic and pointless. Honestly justifying any thought, though, is to know oneself better, and that dive into self-knowledge is important.

I believe I am an artist, in that I view and assess the world through an array of historical artistic creations. Because I am primarily a musical artist, and because music is so uniquely an art and a science, music itself has had a substantial effect on my beliefs over the course of my life.

Science has made extraordinary technological advances in the past century or more; since 1900 the world has changed more than in the totality of recorded history prior to that time. Medical science, for all of its current political entanglements in the United States, is a wonderland of miracles, with cures, vaccinations, preventions, and therapies unimaginable in the nineteenth century. Prior to the technological age, the arts, meaning those human artistic creations that have defined all of history and that exist simply to explain us to ourselves, dwelled in a universe parallel to that of science and other intellectual pursuits; but when science surged forward in the late nineteenth and early twentieth centuries, it left many things behind. Because science has so recently answered many enormous questions—in general, the ones beginning with "How?"—I believe a sizable existential crisis has been created in the arts that mirrors a vaster one going on in our collective psyche, which is trying to either absorb an enormous amount of information or ignore or hide from most of it.

The future relevance of the arts is constantly questioned, particularly in the United States, for the arts do not address the large questions that advance knowledge, those "how" questions. By their nature, the arts traffic in the world of a very different essential question that is never answered except in the privacy of our beliefs, one that has little to do with knowledge: "Why?"

I believe the arts are important because they tell human truths—if not directly in their content, then most certainly in our reactions. I believe artistic abstraction is always the quickest route to emotional reality; through art, we gain understanding of ourselves. Of all of the arts, music is at once the most abstract and the most emotionally accessible. Music is equal parts art and science, fascinating as both; but one needn't understand the science of music to experience it as art, any more than one need understand the atmospheric conditions that set the evening sky ablaze in the west in order to be moved by a sunset. But precisely because music is both an intellectual and an aesthetic pursuit, it is the perfect metaphor for how I believe one must live: with vast respect for provable knowledge and genuine expertise, but never at the expense of the deep joy and wonder of that knowledge, using what can be learned to marvel at what can never be explained.

Music's great gift is that the serious practice of it teaches this with amazing precision, for a musician is forever perfecting the science of the art as well as the art of the science: improving the ear, going deeper into what is already known in search of something as yet unknown, for music never stops undulating with fascinating information. There is never a moment in a musician's life that has a sense of arrival, because each new plateau of knowledge or achievement introduces one to what one cannot yet do or a vast area of repertoire about which one knows almost nothing. Far from being discouraging, this is one of the most appealing things about an artistic life; one awakens every day in anticipation of connecting to it again, in a deeper way than yesterday. Is there a better way to live?

Still, the arts are forever in danger of being sidelined in a world that increasingly feels like it can get along just fine without them. Particularly in tough economic times, any artist can be accused of frivolity, as though attempting to understand the world creatively is unimportant. There are always those who think art is more hobby than profession, and therefore remuneration should be honorary or nonexistent.

This is not to say that exposure to great music is automatically ennobling; many of the upper echelon of Nazis enjoyed Beethoven's symphonies, and more than one despicable despot has loved his Shakespeare. Much less seriously, there is enough duplicitous and abhorrent behavior within the classical arts industry to embarrass us for decades. Nevertheless, the art itself endures beyond these anomalies, and that should induce hope. So much about art is aspirational on some level.

I believe it is of the utmost importance for artists to both perform and live with integrity, probity, accuracy, compassion, and growing knowledge. We too often seek the easiest reward, try to compete with the disposability of pop culture, throw our attention to the loudest person (often the most polished blusterer), and allow our art to become mired in a mediocre shallowness. And yet this is just not good enough for our time, when the world can so easily ignore the greatest of all arts despite their increasing availability. Artists should be working closely together to bring people in, to husband the limited available resources, not making shortsighted decisions of little impact.

I believe very strongly in theory, not simply because we are literally held to the ground by one. Theory is an explanation, not a hypothesis. Music theory, for example, is not a demonstration of what may or may not be true about music; it teaches the qualities of music that are not ephemeral or debatable, those qualities that prove themselves with their own science. For example, the vibrations of a stringed instrument that cause the overtone series would happen exactly the same way anywhere on Earth, in any weather, under any political regime. These overtones can be heard by any ear trained to hear them, but not hearing them does not mean they don't exist or that the theory isn't sound.

Because I view the world through art, and because I know something about the scientific truth of the theory of music, I believe the same must be true with other scientific theories — gravity, relativity, evolution. Just because there is more to learn about them does not negate the extent of what we do and can know. This feels like a constant spiritual lesson.

I believe in arts education, that all children should learn the basics of music, learn to play an instrument, to sing, to recognize Beethoven and Stravinsky. This is not necessarily with the aim of creating more artists in the world, but because an arts education, particularly in music, can teach us to recognize nuance and complexity, both of which are best learned in abstraction, in play. In this way we collect thoughts unconsciously years before we consciously need them, which process results in sounder, more complex thinking. The snap judgments of our sound-bite culture diminish us, and the simplification of complicated realities is a danger to mankind itself. Freedom begins with the ability to think critically and creatively, and the arts can contribute mightily to that. What could possibly be more important for the future of a democracy than the freedom to think?

I believe there is great liberation in having the courage to change one's mind, based on new knowledge or new revelations of old knowledge. My ability to change my mind is rare but accessible proof that I have one.

Artists want to believe that their art has contributed something positive to the world, and I have no doubt that people of religious faith believe that they are bringing a spiritual richness to the world; but we have all witnessed dispiriting and intolerant behavior from both artists and the faithful. And how often in public life have we seen someone declare a belief and then act directly against it? This is an important lesson, for the action is the truer measure of the person. I firmly believe in the morality of the mirror: that each person has a personal responsibility to know what is right and wrong, which can be easily and thrillingly learned from a huge array of historical philosophical perspectives if it is not innately felt.

No art has ever "saved the world" nor helped the world in the same way that a medical or scientific breakthrough does. Because of that, support for the arts in the United States has always been subject to outmoded clichés of class and privilege, since art depends on the largesse of the generous in our country. But although the value of the arts cannot be quantified, I believe that the art of listening is perhaps the most important on Earth; and the arts, particularly serious music, teach us to listen closely, with intent, with intelligence, with pliability, with truth. So the arts may not be lifesaving in a literal sense, but one can certainly say that the world is increasingly dangerous and precipitate owing to a lack of listening, to a lack of the very qualities one might gain from exposure to and immersion in any one of the serious arts.

I believe that sincere gratitude releases creative power, and that empty platitudes are a waste of time.

I believe in the nobility of nature, something I feel expressed most directly in music, in the private sound track of my own life. I believe music was initially invented by man in response to his need to creatively express the omnipresent life force of nature, which is all around us. Nature does not, on its own, make us better, any more than music does; rather, it is the creative contemplation of it, often through art, that allows us to see a deeper and more important nature, that which is within us and has been there all along.

I most strongly believe in and admire anyone for whom art and life are indistinguishable, for whom art is not simply another acquired commodity pasted onto their lives. Oscar Wilde devised the greatest compliment one could deliver to a person: "Life has been your art. You have set yourself to music. Your days are your sonnets."

I believe art to be the true history of a culture, and music is often the capital of our memories. I believe in the integration of the mind and heart: how beautiful are a feeling brain and a thinking soul!

Beliefs are hopeful things, and this is the great gift of music and of a life in the arts, for what in the world is it all for, the great "why," if not for hope? We long so for certainty. Indeed, the current culture seems addicted to it. Music and the arts allow us to safely encounter a world that is more complex than certainty. The wonders of the cosmos should fill us with joy, all of those marvelous things we have yet to know, yet many seem to want an elusive certainty, "truth," right now.

What we never learn how to ask will never be known.

New Harmony

The ancient Chartres labyrinth, versions of which one can find all over the world, has tremendous importance and relevance to music, even relating to classical sonata form in its four quadrants. Mazes and labyrinths have long been a part of spiritual practices, variously in and out of favor with the established religions. Though they are related, mazes and labyrinths differ in a philosophically important way: one can become lost in a maze, and the choices one makes in it affect the length of time it will take you to complete it. This has little relevance to a specifically temporal art like music.

A labyrinth, however, has only one path. The journey is the purpose of its existence; one *cannot* get lost. You enter the labyrinth and are quickly taken near your destination and then far from it, circuitously but with purpose. Because most labyrinths are public spaces, one is rarely alone within one; and encountering others, who most often are strangers, is when one of the great metaphorical meanings of the labyrinth becomes clear. Sometimes you are walking exactly in step with someone else, and then one of you will turn. Sometimes you will come face to face with a person coming from the opposite direction; one must give way. How is that decision made?

The very young often try to complete it in the shortest possible time; it is but another plaything for them. Older participants linger more over their walking time, savoring the possibilities and the lessons with more joy. At Grace Cathedral in San Francisco, for example, home to quite a grand labyrinth in its nave, many tourists, lost in their cameras or phones, walk over it without noticing it, blithely unaware of the congregants actively walking, praying, and meditating all around them. One day a couple watched me walk the labyrinth for a while, staying fully outside of it, each offering their opinions about what I was doing, before the man gruffly and audibly dismissed it all as "pagan bullshit," at which my laughter rang through the empty cathedral.

I was fortunate to find one of the world's most beautiful and peaceful labyrinths in New Harmony, Indiana, a beautifully preserved town on the Wabash River, and a former utopian experiment from the early nineteenth century. This tiny place is the birthplace of modern American geographic studies through its founder, Robert Owen. For several days while contemplating this book, the lectures, and music itself, I found solitude in this extraordinary labyrinth, an experience that is powerful and peaceful in equal measure. Immediate sounds recede, and during the journey through the four quadrants, which can be as slow or fast as one chooses, there is only the sound of one's own footsteps, breathing, and heartbeat.

In the labyrinth, as with our most intimate moments with music, time moves differently; sounds take on a meaning they don't otherwise have. A quiet rhythm emerges.

What, ultimately, is music, and what might its existence prove? It can divert us, challenge us, and make us laugh and cry, but it is more. It makes no difference whether we are speaking of a marvelously crafted humorous song or a glorious opera or symphony lasting many hours. Music surely proves a corresponding reality in us, for it is born out of purest imagination—the making of music is a form of serious play and has a childlike quality to it. Is it not perhaps like gazing into a keyhole, the full reality of which remains mysterious? Because we do not really understand ourselves, our own minds, very well, we are incredibly swift to settle into a definition of ourselves that is less than whole or that accepts thoughts as realities. One of the greatest musicians in history, Leonard Bernstein, said in his essay "The Mountain Disappears" for NPR's *This I Believe*, "If love is the way we have of communicating personally in the deepest way, then what art can do is to extend this communication, magnify it, and carry it to vastly greater numbers of people. Therefore art is valid for the warmth and love it carries within it."

No one wants another trite conclusion that it's all just about love after all. It is about much more than love: for the wonderful traffic cop who loved Verdi (and whose love spared me a ticket), for the deeply gifted child in China, for the many inspiring colleagues and mentors I've encountered in my life, for the composers who conjure creations from the depth of something greater than they knew they possessed—it is about all of them. There is a deeper dimension than love alone, which includes joy, awareness, compassion, empathy. Music may not prove anything about love, science, philosophy, or—to use an outmoded but thoroughly useful word—our souls; but it is also hard to imagine music not gently touching them in some way. We obviously have no way of thinking about ourselves except with our selves. So the questing, joy, pain, love, and laughter that swirl constantly around us, and which illumine the diverse, eccentric passions of this discussion, are felt as music but, like us, are also more. They were called forth by the great creative energy of human beings who left their discoveries behind. I hope that at some deep and important level, we created the art of music because it is the closest to our essence, and that musicians don't want to simply be musicians, they want to be *music*.

> For most of us, there is only the unattended
> Moment, the moment in and out of time,
> The distraction fit, lost in a shaft of sunlight,
> The wild thyme unseen, or the winter lightning,
> Or the waterfall, or music heard so deeply
> That it is not heard at all, but you are the music
> While the music lasts.
> —T. S. Eliot, from "The Dry Salvages" (1941), in *Four Quartets*

ACKNOWLEDGMENTS

I would like to thank Nicholas Shumway, dean of the School of Humanities at Rice University, for his unending support, and Mena Mark Hanna and James Byrne, both on the Houston Grand Opera staff at the time of the lectures, who helped me immensely. The author also gratefully acknowledges the anonymous readers, selected by the editors at the University of Chicago Press, whose astute insights brought these broad ideas into focus. And finally I wish to thank Laura Chandler, the publications editor of the Houston Grand Opera and a close colleague of many years, for her sensitive and elegant editing, which has taught me so much for so long.

Index

Siegfried, 39, 128–29, 130
Siegfried (Wagner), 127
silence, 78
Silent Night (Puts), 138
singing, 6, 15–16, 26–27
Sitwell, Edith, 25
social media, dangers of, 69–70, 74
solitude, 153–54
Sondheim, Stephen, 96, 140
Souls of Black Folk, The (Du Bois), 74
spirit, concept of, 17, 81
"spiritual but not religious" movement, 50–51
spirituality: commonalities with music, 1, 10–11; feeling of personal transformation, 127; as a labyrinth, 96–97; spiritual meanings and experiences, 15, 17–18, 82–83; symbiosis with artistic expression, 41; understanding through music, 42; and wonder, 54, 151. *See also* questioning and openness
St. John Passion (Bach), 2
St. Matthew Passion (Bach), 2, 83–85
Strauss, Richard, 104–5, 107
Styne, Jule, 140
supertitles, 46–47, 120
Susannah (Floyd), 135

Tannhäuser (Wagner), 131
Tartuffe (Mechem), 139
Tchaikovsky, Pyotr, 23
technology. *See* science and technology
Telemann, Georg Philipp, 107
tempo, 25, 111–12, 117, 130–31
Thaïs (Massenet), 140
theory, 96, 148–49
"Thinking Music" (lectures), 12–13
This I Believe series, 144, 154

Tiefland (d'Albert), 140
timbre, 26–27
Tosca (Puccini), 27, 119, 140
transcendence, 1, 17, 45–46
traviata, La (Verdi), 119, 131
Trip to Bountiful, The (Masterson, 1985), 6
Tristan und Isolde (Wagner), 46, 99, 110, 129–30
truth in art and spiritual practices, 6, 19, 54–55, 85, 89, 97, 103
Tsar's Bride, The (Rimsky-Korsakov), 140
Turandot (Puccini), 134, 141–42

United States, religion and spirituality in, 28–31
United States Constitution, 72

Vanessa (Barber), 135
Verdi, Giuseppe, 23, 96, 112; Requiem, 3, 16
vida breve, La (Falla), 140
Village Romeo and Juliet, A (Delius), 140
voice, creative, 6 7
Voss (Meale and Malouf), 139

Wagner, Richard: on conducting, 110–12; the human being and the artist, 112–13; and instrumentation, 106; *Lohengrin*, 3; and man's immortality, 98–99; as metaphor for the twenty-first century, 97; *Parsifal*, 46, 99, 131–32; *Ring des Nibelungen, Der*, 39, 113, 124–27, 128–29, 130, 131; *Tannhäuser*, 131; *Tristan und Isolde*, 46, 99, 110, 129–30
Wagner tubas, 106
Walküre, Die (Wagner), 125
Watkins, Dennis, 139
Weill, Kurt, 140